RAND ARROYO CENTER

Tactical Cyber

Building a Strategy for Cyber Support to Corps and Below

Isaac R. Porche III, Christopher Paul, Chad C. Serena,
Colin P. Clarke, Erin-Elizabeth Johnson, Drew Herrick

Prepared for the United States Army

Approved for public release; distribution unlimited

For more information on this publication, visit www.rand.org/t/RR1600

Library of Congress Cataloging-in-Publication Data is available for this publication.
ISBN: 978-0-8330-9608-1

Published by the RAND Corporation, Santa Monica, Calif.
© Copyright 2017 RAND Corporation
RAND® is a registered trademark.

Cover image by Capt. Meredith Mathis/U.S. Army

www.rand.org

Preface

This report documents research conducted as part of the project "Building a Strategy for Cyber Support to Corps and Below." RAND Arroyo Center was asked by U.S. Army Cyber Command's G35 office to develop and document an Army strategy for providing cyber support to corps and below (CSCB) units that describes how the Army should use its available resources to achieve mission objectives. CSCB is synonymous with *tactical cyber operations*: Both refer to actions in and through the cyberspace domain in support of tactical operations. CSCB is of increasing importance as the Army and other services develop strategies to seamlessly incorporate actions in the cyberspace domain with activities in the traditional warfighting domains (land, air, maritime, and space).

This document proposes a strategy for tactical Army cyber operations. We enumerate overarching goals, objectives, and associated activities. As part of this strategy, we describe what the Army, as an institution, needs to do to realize a vision for tactical cyber operations. In addition, this report discusses the incorporation and use of offensive cyber operations, specifically at the tactical level. Three instructive case studies and lessons from these case studies are presented in this report. This research should be of interest to those involved in developing strategies for Army cyberspace operations, including U.S. Army Cyber Command, U.S. Army Forces Command, U.S. Army Intelligence and Security Command, and First Information Operations Command.

This research was sponsored by U.S. Army Cyber Command and conducted within RAND Arroyo Center's Forces and Logistics Program. RAND Arroyo Center, part of the RAND Corporation, is a federally funded research and development center sponsored by the U.S. Army.

The Project Unique Identification Code (PUIC) for the project that produced this document is HQD156898.

Contents

Figures and Tables

Executive Summary

Future U.S. Army cyber operations will need to be conducted jointly and at all echelons and must include both defensive and offensive components.[1] The Army is now developing doctrine, concepts, and capabilities to conduct and support tactical cyber operations. We propose the following vision statement:

> The Army will be able to employ organic cyber capabilities at the tactical echelon with dedicated personnel in support of tactical units while operating with existing authorities; build trust and operate with joint, interagency, intergovernmental, and multinational (JIIM) partners; and prepare to operate with authorities it might gain in the future to enhance current capabilities.

Based in part on observations from cyber pilot exercises with embedded cyber personnel, tactical units will need to:

- defend tactical assets and key cyber terrain (critical systems, services, and key nodes), including mission command systems, weapon systems, and vehicles
- enable effects through tactical cyber operations.

---

[1] U.S. Army Training and Doctrine Command (TRADOC), "The U.S. Army Operating Concept: Win in a Complex World 2020–2040," TRADOC Pamphlet 525-3-1, October 31, 2014.

Implementation Approach

Three case studies help identify guidelines for implementing this vision and the corresponding goals, especially with regard to tactical cyber operations. These case studies are

1. the experiences of the Joint Interagency Task Force–South (JIATF-S) organization
2. the U.S. Marine Corps' use of signals intelligence (SIGINT) capability at tactical echelons
3. the use of armed drones during Operation Enduring Freedom.

These case studies demonstrate the following best practices toward implementing a strategy for operationalizing tactical cyber operations.

4. **Respect constraints.** Plan to coordinate with higher echelons.
5. **Be patient.** Accept the need to acquire independence, cooperation, access, and other benefits incrementally.
6. **Operate/learn by doing.** Reap the benefits of "doing" at exercises, with JIIM partners and at home station (when brigade combat teams or elements at other tactical levels are not deployed).
7. **Seek win-win.** Have all partners understand "what's in it for me?"
8. **Be there.** Establish and maintain a relationship between personnel who will conduct tactical offensive cyber operations and the partner agencies and organizations with which they will frequently interact.

Not all tactical cyber capability can be part of forward units. We discuss "tethering" as an approach to providing tactical cyber operations capability via reachback. Furthermore, not all offensive cyber capability is practical at the tactical echelon. We define four key factors—proximity, frequency, expertise, and containment of effects—in determining which Army cyber operations are practical at the tactical level.

Summary

The severity and sophistication of cyber threats to U.S. interests, including Department of Defense (DoD) networks, information, and systems, are increasing.[1] Potential enemies are developing offensive cyber capabilities, such as disruptive and destructive malware and antisatellite weapons, designed to interfere with U.S. military communications and computational technologies and freedom of maneuver.[2] And the proliferation of social media, unmanned systems, and other information and communication technologies among adversaries and neutral parties is increasing the complexity of defending U.S. interests from these threats.

The U.S. Army has recognized that cyber operations will need to be conducted jointly and at all echelons, and must include both defensive and offensive components.[3] We propose the following vision statement:

> The Army will be able to employ organic cyber capabilities at the tactical echelon with dedicated personnel in support of tactical units while operating with existing authorities; build trust and

---

[1]   DoD, "Fact Sheet: The Department of Defense (DoD) Cyber Strategy," April 2015a.

[2]   U.S. Army Training and Doctrine Command (TRADOC), "The U.S. Army Operating Concept: Win in a Complex World 2020–2040," TRADOC Pamphlet 525-3-1, October 31, 2014.

[3]   Cyberspace operations are actions at all echelons that generate and exert combat power in and through cyberspace to enable freedom of maneuver and action. The Army as part of the joint team conducts cyberspace operations combined with other nonlethal operations (such as electronic warfare, electromagnetic spectrum operations, and military information support) as well as lethal actions (TRADOC, 2014).

operate with joint, interagency, intergovernmental, and multinational (JIIM) partners; and prepare to operate with authorities it might gain in the future to enhance current capabilities.

Based partly on observations from exercises with embedded cyber personnel, two necessary fundamental cyber capabilities will be (1) defending tactical assets and key terrain, including mission command systems, weapons systems, and vehicles, and (2) enabling effects through tactical offensive cyber operations (OCO). The latter includes the ability to

- collect intelligence by rapidly exploiting captured digital media in a unit's area of operations (AO)
- counter and exploit adversaries' unmanned aerial systems
- protect friendly unmanned aerial systems operating in a unit's AO
- gain access to closed networks in or near a unit's AO
- use electronic warfare systems as "delivery platforms for precision cyber effects"
- prepare to exploit new devices
- conduct cyberspace intelligence, surveillance, and reconnaissance (ISR)
- conduct cyberspace operational preparation of the environment (OPE)
- engage in offensive, defensive, and information-gathering social media operations.[4]

Three case studies are used to identify guidelines for this vision and corresponding goals, especially with regard to tactical cyber operations. We examine the experiences of Joint Interagency Task Force–South (JIATF-S), U.S. Marine Corps (USMC) use of signals intelligence (SIGINT) capability at tactical echelons, and the use of armed drones during Operation Enduring Freedom. This is not an attempt to enumerate all the critical lessons that can be learned from the case

---

[4]   We define *offensive social media operations* as activities conducted directly on social media platforms to gather information, engage in counter-messaging, deliver precision cyber effects, and counter, degrade, deny, or destroy an adversaries' social media operations.

studies. Instead, we highlight what we view to be the most relevant and important implications for tactical OCO.

Case Study One: Joint Interagency Task Force–South

JIATF-S is a multiservice, multiagency task force based at Naval Air Station Key West in Key West, Florida. Its mission is to detect, monitor, and counter illicit trafficking operations and narcoterrorist threats in support of U.S. national and partner-nation security.[5] The task force coordinates with dozens of U.S. and partner-nation agencies and organizations to carry out its mission. To conduct and support tactical cyber operations, the Army will need to similarly coordinate with multiple partners. The lessons from this case inform approaches to standing up organizations and capabilities with multiple partners.

Our examination of JIATF-S activities and conditions offers five lessons relevant to JIIM integration for Army tactical cyber operations. **First, relationship-building takes time.** JIATF-S was neither immediately successful in its mission nor highly integrated with other organizations. Over time, the organization learned how to build relationships: JIATF-S takes the first step of sending a liaison officer (LNO) to a potential partner even before the organization has agreed to reciprocate. As trust and institutional buy-in have strengthened, a tour at JIATF-S has become an attractive experience for both American and international LNOs.

Second, a high operation tempo builds cohesion and provides opportunity for progress. The flow of drug traffic in the JIATF-S area of operations is essentially unceasing, which affords several benefits in terms of building cohesion. Relationships are forged and tested in the crucible of operations, and there are plenty of opportunities to demonstrate success. In addition, JIATF-S pursues so many cases that each JIIM partner sees its objectives advanced frequently enough to value active participation.

---

[5]   JIATF-S, homepage, undated.

Third, understanding and serving each participating organization's equities are crucial. JIATF-S strives to understand and
respect the equities of each organization, involving them in decision-
making and priority setting and protecting their needs for privacy.

**Fourth, collocation increases mutual understanding among
participating organizations.** All JIATF-S staff are in the task force
headquarters, where workspaces are arranged so that staff are constantly being exposed to specific issues of concern to particular participating organizations. At JIATF-S, where turnover is relatively high,
"participants agree there is no real substitute for collocation given the
collaboration requirements of its core activity set."[6]

Fifth, the information-sharing procedures and rules of participating organizations must be accommodated. JIATF-S coordinates and integrates a host of JIIM networks, systems, and capabilities.
Rather than trying to force broad access, JIATF-S employs "man-in-
the-loop" command, control, communications, and computers, in
which participating organizations use their own proprietary resources,
sharing only the information they are allowed to share.

Case Study Two: U.S. Marine Corps Tactical SIGINT

In 2002, the USMC became the first service to receive the resources
and authority necessary to access the nation's SIGINT databases
quickly and efficiently while in theater. The USMC "earned" this
streamlined access in increments from the National Security Agency
(NSA), which controls SIGINT databases, through a combination of
activities, including building and sustaining trust with the agency and
demonstrating the value of the access it was requesting. To conduct
and support tactical cyber operations, the Army will need to earn the
trust of the intelligence community (IC) and the cooperation of law-
enforcement agencies and other partners that might not be initially

---

[6]   Evan Munsing and Christopher J. Lamb, *Joint Interagency Task Force–South: The Best
Known, Least Understood Interagency Success*, Washington, D.C.: National Defense University Press, June 2011, p. 48.

comfortable with the concept of Army OCO. The lessons from this case inform the development of cooperative practices among units and organizations.

The evolution of USMC tactical SIGINT offers five lessons relevant to the Army's goal of conducting and supporting cyber capabilities at all echelons, including tactical echelons. **First, preparation makes it possible to get a foot in the door.** Operation Enduring Freedom brought together two compelling arguments—technology opportunity and circumstance—for requesting streamlined access to the SIGINT databases. The USMC was prepared to seize this opportunity: Its SIGINT community had a longstanding and positive relationship with the NSA, it was aware of what was possible, and it was able to leverage both working and individual relationships.

Second, ongoing operations can demonstrate success and trustworthiness. Early success in using USMC tactical SIGINT to improve results on the battlefield helped the USMC continue to make a case for further relaxation of constraints and for the institutionalization of hitherto provisional or ad hoc access. Strict adherence to initial constraints continually reminded the NSA that its trust in the USMC was not misplaced.

Third, understanding and serving a partner's equities are crucial. By signaling its willingness to accept any and all initial conditions, the USMC adopted an opening negotiation position that clearly subordinated its goals and interests to those of the NSA. Continued "good citizenship," respect for NSA oversight, incremental requests for additional access, and SIGINT Marines' contributions helped the NSA see USMC tactical SIGINT as a net positive.

Fourth, establishing a presence in the partner organization can be instrumental in success. SIGINT Marines were already known to and accepted by the NSA, and the USMC had maintained a USMC SIGINT liaison office at the NSA for many years, which helped convince the NSA to grant SIGINT Marines streamlined access to the SIGINT databases. USMC SIGINT LNOs kept lines of communication open between the USMC and the NSA; ensured that deploying Marines had the access, tools, and training they needed; and helped Marines in the field understand and adhere to NSA policies.

Fifth, accepting conditions unconditionally makes it hard for a partner to say "no." In requesting streamlined access to the SIGINT databases, the USMC agreed to abide by NSA constraints, rules, and oversight requirements. This made it hard for the NSA to change its initial "yes" to a "no."[7]

Case Study Three: The Use of Armed Drones During Operation Enduring Freedom

Both drone warfare and cyber warfare are likely to remain vital in the coming years, as a range of state and nonstate actors, including hybrid adversaries, dominate the international security landscape and threaten the United States and U.S. allies and interests abroad.[8] In the post-9/11 security environment, drone use has outpaced the development and codification of laws designed to govern how drones are used on the battlefield; laws tend to evolve at a slow, deliberate pace, whereas technological innovation occurs very rapidly.[9] This lag has contributed to the already challenging issue of reconciling authorities between the military and the IC. This gap between use and law also applies to cyber warfare.

The debates surrounding armed drones and cyber warfare are occurring in a complex interagency environment that includes Congress, the IC (including the NSA), the White House, and DoD, among others. There is also a growing domestic debate over the moral, legal, and ethical use of these new technologies. Nevertheless, the use of both technologies continues to accelerate. It seems clear that the rapid growth of both the threat and U.S. capability is clearing a path through the legal complexities. The challenges and opportunities surrounding the

---

[7]   Cynthia Dion-Schwarz, personal communication with the author, April 4, 2016.

[8]   Patrick B. Johnston and Annop K. Sarbahi, "The Impact of U.S. Drone Strikes on Terrorism in Afghanistan and Pakistan," *International Studies Quarterly,* Vol. 60, No. 2, 2016, pp. 203–219.

[9]   Jason Andress and Steven Winterfeld, *Cyber Warfare: Techniques, Tactics and Tools for Security Practitioners*, Waltham, Mass.: Syngress, 2011, p. 209.

use of armed drones provide instruction and optimism for the Army's tactical OCO. A famous catchphrase applies: "If you build it, they [the authorities] will come."

Most of the lessons from case studies one and two concern the issue of organizational adaptation, whereas case study three's are more relevant to tactical employability. However, the case of armed drones does offer lessons relevant to organization. **First, in spite of the lack of clear lines of jurisdiction and responsibility, operational necessity resulted in multiple high-level authorizations**. To disrupt the al Qaida network and its regional affiliates across the world, the United States went on the offensive and learned by doing.

Second, there is a need to recognize the importance of working with local partners. This can only be done by liaising and having a forward presence, however limited, where a robust intelligence apparatus on the ground can provide context to an otherwise anarchic and fluid situation and potentially mitigate collateral damage.[10]

Authorities Issues

The authority required to conduct tactical OCO will continue to be managed and granted deliberately by strategic and operational echelons in the near term. As case study three highlights, concerns regarding collateral damage, blowback, deconfliction, attribution, and proportionality will have to be addressed for any capability developed. Furthermore, any capability employed might need to be preceded by a significant need to collect intelligence. For these reasons, higher echelons must be involved with the application of OCO, along with key partners (e.g., organizations with Title 50 authorizations).

Case study three is also instructive with respect to opportunities to take advantage of new capabilities, tactics, techniques, procedures, etc., especially with respect to counterinsurgency operations. Concerns

---

[10] Christopher Paul, Jennifer D. P. Moroney, Beth Grill, Colin P. Clarke, Lisa Saum-Manning, Heather Peterson, and Brian Gordon, *What Works Best When Building Partner Capacity in Challenging Contexts?* Santa Monica, Calif.: RAND Corporation, RR-937-OSD, 2015.

(perceived and real limitations on authorities, concerns about blowback, controlling for proportionality, and other challenges usually managed at the strategic echelon) surrounding USMC use of tactical SIGINT were overcome; similar concerns surrounding tactical OCO could also be surmounted using similar processes. For instance, new cyber threats are continuing to emerge, cyber operational capabilities are being developed, and mission needs are changing, which could lead to pressures to establish new authorities for tactical OCO. In any case, the successful use of SIGINT capability in Operation Enduring Freedom projects an opportunity to do the same for certain offensive cyber capabilities.

An Approach for Army Tactical OCO: Tethering

Army strategists and planners (and the U.S. military more broadly) are thinking about possible authorities changes that could afford tactical forces more flexibility in the conduct of cyber operations. In the interim, while authority to conduct tactical OCO rests at higher echelons, one approach that could facilitate OCO at tactical levels comes from an unlikely source: Hollywood. In James Cameron's 1986 film *Aliens*, a marine private performs a cyber-electronic attack with specialized equipment while receiving support from a reachback facility. This could be used as a model for Army tactical OCO, in which remotely supported cyber operators perform activities at tactical levels with reachback support. Indeed, in describing a "way ahead for tactical cyber," U.S. Army Cyber Commander LTG Edward C. Cardon suggested that "small cyberteams could be attached to brigades or lower level units. These teams would be 'tethered' back to national-level agencies for the sake of obtaining authorization to act."[11]

A great number of the operations in, through, or in support of operations in cyberspace can be accomplished remotely. These operations can be conducted virtually anywhere and by anyone with the proper authorities, training, equipment, and relationships with JIIM

---

[11] Joe Gould, "Ground Commanders with Cyber Skills," *Army Times*, July 1, 2014.

partners. The Army provides the connection and coordination necessary to ensure that these remote operations are available to commanders on the ground.

An Approach to Determining What Types of Tactical OCO Are Practical

Four factors help determine which tactical OCO are practical: proximity, frequency, expertise, and containment of effects. *Proximity* refers
to how physically close a soldier needs to get to a target to perform a
cyber operation. *Frequency* references how often a tactical unit, such
as a brigade combat team (BCT), expects to perform a cyber operation. *Expertise* refers to the degree to which highly trained experts are
required to conduct the cyber operation. *Containment* (of effects) refers
to the ability to keep effects within a bounded area for a predetermined
duration. The flowchart presented in Figure S.1 shows how answering
questions related to these four key factors can help determine whether
a tactical OCO is practical. However, there are intangibles and unfore-
seen events that might not provide an answer in the flowchart.

Best Practices, Important Considerations, and Associated Recommendations

Each of the three case studies described in this report was selected to
illuminate one of the following three overarching OCO requirements.

- The Army must be able to operate with JIIM partners (case study one).
- The Army must be able to use cyber capabilities at all echelons, including tactical echelons (case study two).
- The Army must be able to operate with existing authorities and prepared to operate with authorities it might gain in the future (case study three).

Figure S.1
Flowchart to Assess Practical Tactical Offensive Cyber Capability

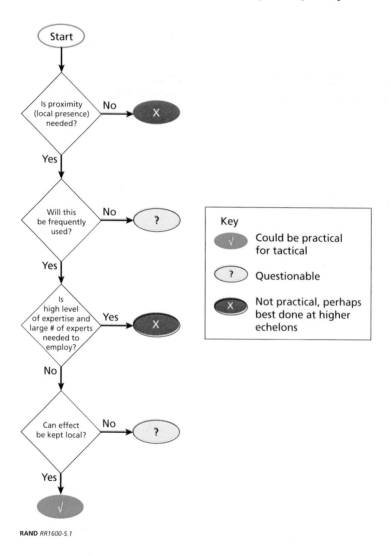

RAND RR1600-S.1

Taken together, the lessons learned from the case studies suggest five best practices for the Army as it develops and implements the ability to conduct and support tactical OCO.

1. **Respect constraints.** Plan to coordinate with higher echelons until authorities for tactical OCO are clarified and, potentially, devolved to lower echelons and partner agencies/nations.

2. **Be patient.** Accept the need to acquire independence, cooperation, access, and other benefits incrementally rather than instantaneously when working with JIIM partners. Incremental steps and success are self-reinforcing and will build on each other over time.

3. **Operate/learn by doing.** Find creative ways for reaping the benefits of "doing" with JIIM partners when BCTs (or elements at other tactical levels) are not deployed.

4. **Seek win-win.** When approaching a partner, make the value proposition explicit, so that the partner does not wonder, "What's in it for me?"

5. **Be there.** When considering how best to embed capability at tactical echelons, identify how to establish and maintain a relationship between the personnel who will serve at those echelons and the partner agencies and organizations with which they will interact frequently.

Acknowledgments

We thank our sponsors at U.S. Army Cyber Command for providing guidance and direction. Key staff include Ron Pontius, COL Landy T. Nelson, LTC Cade Saie, LTC Christopher Fahrenbach, and MAJ Matthew Funk. Personnel from the USMC NSA liaison office provided insights used in our report, including a detailed account of the history of the relationship between NSA and USMC signals intelligence. We owe a similar debt of gratitude to the more than 20 individuals assigned to Joint Interagency Task Force–South (JIATF-S) with whom we spoke. We are also indebted to former JIATF-S commander RADM Joe Nimmich, who provided us with additional background on JIATF-S and his understanding of how and why it works.

Key personnel at U.S. Army Intelligence and Security Command, the Army G-2 office, and the Army War College spent significant time providing us with insights and observations into the complexities of policy issues. They include William ("Joe") Thompkins, Alfred ("Al") Monteiro Jr., CW5 Al Mollenkopf, Mark. S. Sanford, Sr., Raymond C. Perkins, CPT Jennifer D. Norvell, Michael Fox, and David Mayfield.

LTC Jon Burnett, LTC Pam Tindal, and CPT Leander Metcalf shared key reports and facilitated numerous interviews with participants in a number of the cyber pilot efforts.

In addition, COL Michael York made contributions to this report as a RAND Army Fellow, as did Tom Curley. LTG (Ret.) Rhett Hernandez provided comments on an early draft of this report that helped shape this current version. We would also like to extend our thanks to Brian Wisniewski and Cynthia Diaz-Schwarz for their thorough and thoughtful reviews. Morten Bay made important contributions to the chapter on social media operations. Finally, the authors greatly appreciate the administrative support provided by Michelle McMullen, who helped format and review this draft.

Abbreviations

AAR	after-action report
AO	area of operations
AR	Army Regulation
ASCC	Army Service Component Command
BCT	brigade combat team
C2	command and control
C4	command, control, communications, and computers
CIA	Central Intelligence Agency
CPB	Cyber Protection Brigade
CREW	counter-radio electronic warfare
CSCB	cyber support to corps and below
DCO	defensive cyberspace operations
DoD	Department of Defense
DOTMLPF-P	doctrine, organization, training, materiel, leadership, personnel, facilities and policy
DSMO	defensive social media operations
EMIB	Expeditionary Military Intelligence Brigade

EO	Executive Order
EW	electronic warfare
FM	field manual
IC	intelligence community
IED	improvised explosive device
IGSMO	information-gathering social media operations
IP	Internet Protocol
ISR	intelligence, surveillance, and reconnaissance
JCCC	Joint Cyber Component Command
JIATF-S	Joint Interagency Task Force–South
JIIM	joint, interagency, intergovernmental, and multinational
JP	Joint Publication
JRTC	Joint Readiness Training Center
JTF	Joint Task Force
LESI	law-enforcement sensitive information
LNO	liaison officer
NATO	North Atlantic Treaty Organization
NSA	National Security Agency
OCO	offensive cyber operations
OPE	operational preparation of the environment
OPFOR	opposing forces
OPSEC	operational security

OSMO	offensive social media operations
RSCO	remotely supported cyber operator
RSTB	Ranger Special Troops Battalion
S2	intelligence
S6	signals
SCIF	Sensitive Compartmented Information Facility
SIGINT	signals intelligence
SMO	social media operations
TRADOC	U.S. Army Training and Doctrine Command
TTP	tactics, techniques, and procedures
UAS	unmanned aerial system
USMC	United States Marine Corps
USP	U.S. Person

CHAPTER ONE

Understanding the U.S. Army's Need for Tactical Offensive Cyber Operations

Cyberspace

Joint doctrine describes three layers of cyberspace: the physical network layer, the logical network layer, and the cyber-persona layer (as depicted in Figure 1.1).[1] Each one of these layers has a presence at the tactical echelon.

Figure 1.1
The Three Layers of Cyberspace

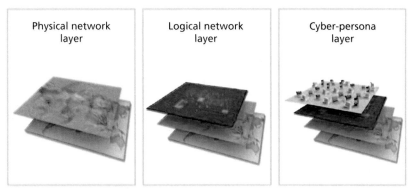

SOURCE: Department of Defense, *Cyberspace Operations*, Joint Publication JP 3-12 (R), February 5, 2013.
RAND *RR1600-1.1*

---

[1] DoD, *Cyberspace Operations*, Joint Publication (JP) 3-12 (R), February 5, 2013.

Failing to fully consider these three elements of cyberspace and the interactions among them will undermine development of cyber operations. This report includes key recommendations that directly address these layers and their intersection with tactical offensive cyber operations.

Why Tactical Cyber Operations?

The Army—and by extension, Army brigade combat teams (BCTs)—rely on information technology to support many tasks and have an ever-increasing dependence on cyberspace. In the future, BCTs will be responsible for areas of operations (AOs) that are not only dense with people, but full of various information technologies and volumes of digitally stored and transmitted data (e.g., "Big Data"). Advancements in information technology will require BCTs to operate in environments that contain adversaries who can perform cyber operations both cheaply and easily. A brigade commander will need to respond with sufficient speed to such events in what is likely to be a dynamic, information-rich environment. Even at the brigade level, all the layers of cyberspace—physical devices (e.g., cyber assets), logical connections, and adversarial actors—have to be managed. Tactical cyber operations have received significantly increased attention over the last year, partly due to these management issues.

In its February 2010 *Cyberspace Operations Concept Capability Plan*, the U.S. Army described its need for cyber operations at tactical levels (i.e., corps and below)—a need driven primarily by the "rapidly changing nature of cyberspace," which mandates that operational and tactical units possess organic, or have access to, the capabilities and expertise to protect these vital networks; enable real time attack prevention and detection; make possible attack response through event identification and actions such as deception, blocking and/or denying; and allow the coordination of appropriate attacks.[2]

---

[2]   U.S. Army Training and Doctrine Command (TRADOC), "United States Army Cyberspace Operations Concept Capability Plan 2016–2028," Pamphlet 525-7-8, February 22, 2010, p. 20.

The Army is beginning to experiment with the conduct of tactical cyber operations by incorporating their use—including at the brigade level—during unit rotations at combat training centers.[3] The Army's hope is that this "experimentation might clear up confusion in the DoD about how to wage cyberwarfare at the tactical level."[4]

Opportunities for Offensive Cyber Operations

Today, adversaries use available, open information and communications technologies to operate. In the future, the proliferation of electronics, such as appliances that are part of the "Internet of Things" and networked vehicles (see Appendix), will provide more targets of opportunity. These opportunities have been considered as part of the Army's cyber pilot projects. In Joint Readiness Training Center (JRTC) exercises, tactical units have considered ways to mitigate adversaries that use social media and the Internet to gather intelligence about U.S. forces. During the exercises, U.S. forces pursued ways of intelligence-gathering and sharing through social media and the Internet. These exercises are good examples of battlefield-relevant offensive cyber operations (OCO).[5]

A recent article offered another example of the necessity of tactical-level OCO.[6] The article highlighted how the growing use of net-

---

[3] Joe Gould, "Ground Commanders with Cyber Skills," *Army Times*, July 1, 2014.

[4] Gould, 2014.

[5] At the January 2016 cyber pilot held at NTC, the training facility included

> replicating a real-world network provider serving the several mock villages in the box, establishing wifi access points and providing laptops and smartphones to enable online communication. Soldiers acting as opposing forces and "cyber threat actors"—role-players simulating civilians on the battlefield or enemy sympathizers—can use the system to do everything from carry on routine conversations to help adversary forces target U.S. Soldiers. The same network also enables friendly forces to detect and take action against threats (U.S. Army Cyber Command, "Integration of Cyberspace Capabilities into Tactical Units," Army.mil, 2016).

[6] Alfred C. Crane and Richard Peeke, "Using the Internet of Things to Gain and Maintain Situational Awareness in Dense Urban Environments and Mega Cities," *Small Wars Journal*, February 26, 2016.

worked embedded systems in not only traditional industrial automa-
tion applications (power distribution, elevators, water treatment, etc.)
but in commercial and consumer applications (FitBits, smart phones,
traffic management, etc.) dramatically expands the cyber battlespace
available to a supported commander.[7]

The Challenges of Tactical Operations
More broadly, the Army has stated that future cyber operations must
be conducted jointly and at all echelons, and they must include both
defensive and offensive components.[8] Doctrine and concepts are being
developed to support this projection. Through three case studies and
observations at exercises and training events, this report identifies the
following lessons that can inform Army efforts to develop its ability to
conduct tactical OCO.

- The Army must be able to build trust with the intelligence community (IC) and operate with joint, interagency, intergovernmental, and multinational (JIIM) partners.
- The Army must be able to employ cyber capabilities at all echelons, including tactical echelons.
- The Army must be able to operate with existing authorities and
  prepared to operate with authorities it might gain in the future.

Disadvantages of the Tactical Environment

Several factors combine to create a unique cyber environment at the
tactical level. Tactical networks have limited bandwidth. They also
have high bit error rates, high latency, and intermittent connectivity,

---

[7]   Brian Wisniewski, personal communication with the author, February 29, 2016.

[8]   "Army commanders must protect their own systems and disrupt the enemy's ability to
operate. Army units will have to operate with degraded communications and reduced access
to cyber and space capabilities. Army forces will have to support joint operations through
reconnaissance, offensive operations or raids to destroy land-based enemy space and cyberspace capabilities" (TRADOC, "The U.S. Army Operating Concept: Win in a Complex
World 2020–2040," TRADOC Pamphlet 525-3-1, October 31, 2014).

and both the users and the infrastructure are mobile. Mission command data pass through these channels. Additional security measures often create additional data-flow challenges. The distributed nature of Army tactical networks, combined with adversary proximity, makes it easier for an adversary to intercept communications. This problem is exacerbated when tactical units are within an adversary's radio line of sight (although this can be an advantage, as the adversary is also vulnerable in this situation).[9]

Examples of Potential Requirements for Tactical OCO

Cyber operational capability at tactical levels is not new. As reporter Joe Gould notes,

> a [BCT] has a number of systems already in place to help a commander gain intel in a cyberspace environment. That includes the ability to map adversary networks, identify potential vulnerabilities and perform counter-recon to either confuse or deny hacking attempts.[10]

However, future tactical OCO will have to account for the growing complexities—and opportunities—inherent in tomorrow's battlespace. The severity and sophistication of cyber threats to U.S. interests, including DoD networks, information, and systems, are increasing.[11] Potential adversaries are developing offensive cyber capabilities—such as disruptive and destructive malware and antisatellite weapons—designed to interfere with U.S. military communications and freedom of maneuver, and the proliferation of social media, unmanned systems, and other technologies among adversaries and

---

[9] Kristen Kushiyama, "Army to Focus on Cyber Strategy in Tactical Environments," CERDEC Public Affairs, May 11, 2015.

[10] Gould, 2014.

[11] DoD, "Fact Sheet: The Department of Defense (DoD) Cyber Strategy," April 2015a.

neutral parties increases the complexity of defending U.S. interests.[12] Tactical OCO might involve the following actions, some of which span different functional areas (e.g., intelligence, operational security [OPSEC]):

- rapidly exploiting captured digital media
- countering (and exploiting) unmanned aerial systems (UAS) by exploiting data feeds or absconding with or coopting a UAS
- protecting friendly UASs
- gaining access to closed networks in or near a unit's AO, including extracting and injecting data[13]
- using electronic warfare systems as "delivery platforms for precision cyber effects"[14]
- exploiting new devices emerging from new trends and opportunities[15]

---

[12] TRADOC, 2014.

[13] Zachary Fryer-Biggs, "DoD Looking to 'Jump the Gap' into Adversaries' Closed Networks," *Defense News*, January 15, 2013.

[14] Kristen Kushiyama, "Army Looks to Blend Cyber, Electronic Warfare Capabilities on Battlefield," Army.mil, October 29, 2013.

[15] The proliferation of information technology and wired and wireless connectivity will present new opportunities in the future, especially with regard to the "Internet of Things." As noted by Isaac Porche, Jerry Sollinger, and Shawn McKay, "As long as a device is not dumb (that is, as long as it contains a processor and some memory), it can be accessed, affected, and controlled to some degree by anyone who can overcome the air gap" (Porche, Sollinger, and McKay, *A Cyberworm That Knows No Boundaries*, Santa Monica, Calif.: RAND Corporation, OP-342-OSD, 2011). Megacities will be future operating areas for ground forces that will likely encounter appliances and automobiles in abundance, all of which present exploitation opportunities (Edward Markey and staff, *Tracking and Hacking: Security & Privacy Gaps Put American Drivers at Risk*, U.S. Senate report, February 2015; Isaac Porche, "The Myth of Cyber Defense: What Happens When the Worm Turns," presented at Cyberspace: Malevolent Actors, Criminal Opportunities and Strategic Competition, Panel II: Strategic Competition in Cyberspace Part 2, University of Pittsburgh, November 1–2, 2012; Porche, Sollinger, and McKay, 2011; Karl Koscher, Alexei Czeskis, Franziska Roesner, et al., "Experimental Security Analysis of a Modern Automobile," presented at IEEE Symposium on Security and Privacy, May 16–19, 2010, in Oakland, Calif.; and Isaac Porche, "The Threat from Inside . . . Your Automobile," in Phil Williams and Dighton Fiddner, eds., *Cyberspace: Malevolent Actors, Criminal Opportunities, and Strategic Competition*, Carlisle, Pa.: U.S. Army War College Press, 2016).

- conducting cyberspace intelligence, surveillance, and reconnaissance (ISR)[16]
- conducting cyberspace operational preparation of the environment (OPE)[17]
- engaging in offensive social media operations (OSMO).[18]

Chapters Two, Three, and Four describe the three case studies:

1. the evolution of Joint Interagency Task Force–South (JIATF-S) and its organization
2. U.S. Marine Corps use of signals intelligence (SIGINT) at the tactical level
3. the use of armed drones during Operation Enduring Freedom.

Chapter Five describes lessons from the Army's recent cyber pilots at the JRTC. Chapter Six focuses on the emerging role that social media plays in cyber operations. Chapter Seven describes an approach for providing tactical OCO. Chapter Eight outlines a means of determining what types of OCO are practical at tactical levels. Chapter Nine is a summary chapter that highlights best practices, important consider-

---

[16] "An intelligence action conducted by the JFC authorized by an EXORD or conducted by attached SIGINT units under temporary delegated SIGINT operational tasking authority. Cyberspace ISR includes ISR activities in cyberspace conducted to gather intelligence that may be required to support future operations, including OCO or DCO. These activities synchronize and integrate the planning and operation of cyberspace systems, in direct support of current and future operations. Cyberspace ISR focuses on tactical and operational intelligence and on mapping adversary cyberspace to support military planning" (Department of the Army, *Field Manual 3-12: Cyberspace and Electronic Warfare Operations*, Washington, D.C.: Headquarters, Department of the Army, forthcoming).

[17] "Cyberspace [operational preparation of the environment (OPE)] consists of the nonintelligence enabling activities conducted to plan and prepare for potential follow-on military operations. Cyberspace OPE requires forces trained to a standard that prevents compromise of related intelligence collection operations" (DoD, *Field Manual 3-38: Cyber Electromagnetic Activities*, Washington, D.C.: Headquarters, Department of the Army, January 30, 2013).

[18] OSMO includes activities conducted directly on social media platforms to gather information, engage in counter-messaging, deliver precision cyber effects, and counter, degrade, deny, or destroy adversaries' social media operations.

ations, and associated recommendations for the Army. We conclude with a general strategy for the Army to follow to enable the conduct of tactical cyber operations.

CHAPTER TWO

Case Study One: Joint Interagency Task Force–South

To conduct and support tactical OCO, the Army will need to coordinate with multiple partners. This chapter examines JIATF-S as a case study of an organization that conducts "highly coordinated, seamless operations" with a very wide variety of partners.[1] JIATF-S coordinates with dozens of U.S. and partner-nation agencies and organizations to carry out its mission of countering illicit trafficking and narcoterrorist threats. It is "well known within the U.S. government as the 'gold standard' for interagency cooperation and intelligence fusion."[2]

An Introduction to Joint Interagency Task Force–South

JIATF-S is a multiservice, multiagency task force based at Naval Air Station Key West in Key West, Florida. Its mission is to detect, monitor, and counter illicit trafficking operations and narcoterrorist threats in support of U.S. national and partner-nation security.[3]

In pursuit of this mission, JIATF-S works with U.S. military forces drawn from four U.S. combatant commands and with the U.S.

---

[1] Federation of American Scientists Intelligence Resource Program, "Counterdrug," web page, January 4, 1998.

[2] Evan Munsing and Christopher J. Lamb, *Joint Interagency Task Force–South: The Best Known, Least Understood Interagency Success*, Washington, D.C.: National Defense University Press, June 2011, p. 1.

[3] JIATF-S, homepage, undated.

Coast Guard. It also works with more than a dozen domestic agencies and collaborates directly with more than a dozen foreign nations, most of which have contributed one or more full-time liaison officers (LNOs) to JIATF-S and some of which have contributed forces directly to JIATF-S. This is a partial list of the broad range of organizations that participate in JIATF-S:

- U.S. military services: Air Force, Army, Marine Corps, Navy, Coast Guard[4]
- U.S. law-enforcement agencies: Customs and Border Protection, Drug Enforcement Agency (DEA), Federal Bureau of Investigations
- U.S. intelligence agencies: Central Intelligence Agency (CIA), Defense Intelligence Agency, National Reconnaissance Office, National Geospatial-Intelligence Agency, National Security Agency (NSA)
- Other U.S. agencies: Department of Justice, Department of Transportation
- Partner nations: Argentina, Brazil, Canada, Chile, Colombia, Dominican Republic, Ecuador, El Salvador, France, Mexico, Netherlands, Peru, United Kingdom.

Despite this host of participating organizations, JIATF-S functions smoothly, interdicting more narcotics and supporting more trafficking convictions than any of its predecessor organizations.

However, JIATF-S has not always been so successful in fulfilling its mission or so highly integrated with other organizations. JIATF-S's predecessor organizations were established more than 20 years ago, and initially faced challenges. In its first incarnation in 1989, the organization now known as JIATF-S consisted of three Joint Task Forces (JTFs): JTF 4, JTF 5, and JTF 6. These JTFs were purely military organizations charged with combating the flow of drugs from Colombia.

As purely military organizations, the three JTFs had no law-enforcement authority—a condition that led to many incidents of insti-

---

[4]   The Coast Guard has law-enforcement authority as well.

tutional and bureaucratic conflict. Prospective participating organizations were neither required to coordinate with the JTFs nor particularly encouraged to do so. As a long-serving JIATF-S civilian explains, "For the first five years, we had to find things to do, and then ask forgiveness." Poor relationships with prospective participating organizations and a lack of necessary law-enforcement authority made the JTFs an expensive and inefficient use of government assets.

The first U.S. National Interdiction Command and Control Plan, signed in 1994 by the director of the Office of National Drug Control Policy and still in use today, was a progressive piece of national-level guidance that established three geographically oriented counterdrug JIATFs.[5] These three task forces were ultimately merged into what is now JIATF-S.

The transformation from JTF to JIATF created the conditions that make possible JIATF-S's coordination with multiple organizations. But the transformation was neither automatic nor swift. It involved many missteps and false starts. As the same long-serving JIATF-S affiliate explains, "It took 22 years to get here—to achieve truly integrated, synchronized, interagency and international counterdrug operations."

Activities That Contribute to the Task Force's Success

JIATF-S's "highly coordinated, seamless operations" often involve feats of JIIM integration that have become a routine part of operations.[6] We identified six JIATF-S activities that contribute to the task force's success.

Integrating Intelligence, Assets, and Authorities
As the following description of a typical JIATF-S case shows, JIATF-S operations are driven by actionable intelligence that flows into the task force. JIAFT-S then draws on assets from a range of sources to coordinate the surveillance, interception, boarding, and search of ves-

---

[5]   Federation of American Scientists Intelligence Resource Program, 1998.

[6]   Federation of American Scientists Intelligence Resource Program, 1998.

sels, as well as any subsequent law-enforcement action that immediately follows.

A typical case can start with JIATF-S receiving actionable law-enforcement information from the U.S. Drug Enforcement Administration. This prompts the deployment of a U.S. Customs and Border Protection P-3 or a U.S. Coast Guard C-130 that subsequently detects and monitors a foreign-flagged suspect vessel until JIATF-S can sortie a U.S. Coast Guard cutter or U.S. Navy or allied surface ship with an embarked Law-Enforcement Detachment to intercept. When that ship arrives on scene, tactical control shifts from JIATF-S to the U.S. Coast Guard. In the case of a foreign-flagged suspect vessel, the U.S. Coast Guard tactical commander implements a bilateral agreement or arrangement in force with the vessel's flag state to confirm registry and to stop, board, and search the vessel for drugs. If drugs are found, jurisdiction and disposition over the vessel, drugs and crew are coordinated with the U.S. Department of State, the U.S. Department of Justice, and the flag state.[7]

In many cases, JIATF-S fuses intelligence from multiple sources and draws on both U.S. and partner-nation assets for operations. Because most countries (including the United States) separate military and law-enforcement functions, the presence of appropriate law-enforcement personnel is arranged to legitimize arrests and increase the likelihood of successful prosecutions. In fact, although JIATF-S military assets operate exclusively under U.S. Code Title 10 authorities, JIATF-S can integrate into its operations participating organizations that have authorities under Titles 3 (The President), 8 (Aliens and Nationality), 14 (Coast Guard), 18 (Crimes and Criminal Procedure), 19 (Customs Duties), 21 (Food and Drugs), 32 (National Guard), and 50 (War and National Defense).[8]

---

[7]   Wayne E. Justice, "Overview of Coast Guard Drug and Migrant Interdiction," testimony before the House Committee on Transportation and Infrastructure, Subcommittee on Coast Guard and Maritime Transportation, March 18, 2009.

[8]   Title 10–Title 50 discussions are essentially a debate about the proper roles and missions of U.S. military forces and intelligence agencies. "Title 10" is used colloquially to refer to DoD and military operations, while "Title 50" refers to intelligence agencies, intelligence activities, and covert action (Andru Wall, "Demystifying the Title 10–Title 50 Debate:

Mixing and Matching Capabilities and Authorities

The strength of JIATF-S, according to former JIATF-S commander RADM Joe Nimmich, is the ability to mix and match capabilities and authorities to optimize the operational effectiveness of assets. One example is placing a law-enforcement detachment aboard a U.S. Navy warship. With a law-enforcement detachment on board, arrest and investigative authority can be projected where needed.

Employing Minimalist Doctrine for Tactical Control

JIATF-S employs a uniquely minimalist doctrine. It does not use memoranda of understanding; rather, most of the requirements for operational coordination are covered within standing operating procedures. Organizations that contribute forces to JIATF-S (including four U.S. combatant commands, the U.S. Coast Guard, and various U.S. interagency organizations) grant tactical control of specific assets for extended durations directly to JIATF-S. This means that JIATF-S can "move assets around its operating area like chess pieces."[9] Partner-nation organizations retain tactical control of their assets but, during operating periods, post LNOs on the JIATF-S operations floor.

On the JIATF-S joint interagency intelligence operations center floor, representatives from every participating organization sit with their own national or home organization systems and provide "tear line"[10] input into the shared JIATF-S system. Personnel at various interagency participating organizations also sit right next to each other (e.g., an NSA LNO will sit next to a DEA LNO). Each participating organization's representative protects the equities of his or her agency but, through sharing physical space with other participating organizations, manages to share the information needed for situational awareness.

Distinguishing Military Operations, Intelligence Activities, and Covert Action," *Harvard National Security Journal*, Vol. 3, No. 1, September 2011, pp. 85–142).

[9]   Munsing and Lamb, 2011, p. 37.

[10]   "Tear line" is intelligence jargon that refers to a portion of a sheet of paper or a report that can be less restricted as to who can see it. It is a manual means to segregate sensitive data.

Sharing Sensitive Information

Sharing classified intelligence data is not, according to JIATF-S person-nel, the task force's biggest challenge. Although the rules that govern the sharing and transmission of classified data are strict (especially in the case of data-sharing with partner nations), the rules are consistent. Once an exception (e.g., granting certain partner-nation representa-tives a security clearance) is requested and approved, these exceptions become routine procedures understood by everyone in the task force.

The real challenge is "law-enforcement sensitive" information (LESI). Although this information is not formally classified, its dis-tribution is controlled by the law-enforcement officer who "owns" it. Whereas sharing classified information with unauthorized parties is illegal, sharing LESI incurs no legal penalty. However, any law-enforcement officer who shares information beyond the scope explic-itly permitted by the controlling case officer would immediately and irrevocably lose the trust of that case officer. Precisely who can receive specific LESI varies from case officer to case officer, so protecting LESI is nowhere near as straightforward as protecting classified data. JIATF-S meets this challenge on a case-to-case basis and by using per-son-to-person transfers of information; close proximity helps.

Developing Close Relationships with Participating Organizations

JIATF-S has developed close working relationships with all of its par-ticipating organizations. To initiate relationships, JIATF-S sends an LNO to a prospective participating organization even before that orga-nization has agreed to reciprocate with its own LNO. Once the partici-pating organization reciprocates by sending an LNO, JIATF-S embeds that organization's personnel in the task force's senior staff. The fact that the senior staff (i.e., the various "J-codes" and their deputies) is peppered with personnel from participating organizations makes it abundantly clear that JIATF-S is a truly interagency organization. Fur-thermore, LNOs do more than just liaise: They are active members of the JIATF-S team and participate in daily activities.

Protecting the Equities of Participating Organizations

According to JIATF-S staff, the task force's primary management challenge is balancing the equities of all the various participating organizations. Balancing equities means ensuring that the goals and objectives of each participating organization are pursued—and met—as often as possible. JIATF-S "makes every effort to take into account" participating organizations' "policies, directives, rules of engagement and legal authorities and constraints."[11] This gives every participating organization a positive stake in JIATF-S, ensures high levels of participation and sharing, and makes it possible for JIATF-S to sustain its level of JIIM integration.

Conditions That Contribute to the Task Force's Success

These six JIATF-S activities are not, in and of themselves, sufficient to explain the task force's success. Underlying these activities are seven important conditions that make these activities possible.

A Shared, Clear, Unitary Goal

Each organization that participates in JIATF-S shares a common vision, mission, and purpose: combating illicit trafficking. According to JIATF-S staff, this clear shared goal is central to the task force's success, helping team members "transcend the competing cultures of their home agencies and . . . unify the efforts of people with very different backgrounds and experiences."[12] Each participating organization also acknowledges that working with others in a coordinated, integrated fashion improves its own ability to advance its organizational or national counter trafficking objectives.

Voluntary Participation

Participating organizations are under no legal or other formal obligation to cooperate with JIATF-S; they do so of their own volition.

---

[11] Munsing and Lamb, 2011, p. 47.

[12] Munsing and Lamb, 2011, p. 35.

Indeed, participating organizations "pay their own way" by bearing the cost of posting LNOs to JIATF-S. This means that every participating organization has calculated that cooperation with JIATF-S is worth the cost.

Clear Benefits to Cooperation

As noted earlier, each participating JIATF-S organization understands that cooperation yields clear benefits over working alone. These benefits include increased mission effectiveness, intelligence sharing, and the development of partnerships and relationships that might extend into other areas. The benefits to participating organizations are sufficient to keep the organizations involved and make them unwilling to jeopardize the connections they have forged and the benefits they reap.

JIATF-S is also generous in acknowledging the contributions of individuals and participating organizations, who "know they will be given due credit for their efforts."[13] Indeed, participating organizations believe they get "a great return on their investment. In exchange for intelligence, personnel, funding, aircraft, or other assets, they get credit for drug seizures or prosecutions," making a partnership with JIATF-S a productive undertaking.[14]

Cooperative Decisionmaking and Priority-Setting

As noted earlier, JIATF-S has been successful in balancing the equities of the participating organizations. Critical to this balance is ensuring that participating organizations share in decisionmaking and setting priorities. At JIATF-S,

> strategic decisions are collaboratively made by a command team consisting of the director, vice director, deputy director, senior liaisons, and the heads of the J-staff, although particularly important decisions may require the input of a group of as many as

---

[13]   Munsing and Lamb, 2011, p. 45.

[14]   Munsing and Lamb, 2011, p. 45.

20 to 30 people, including representatives from all participating organizations.[15]

The task force's institutional culture includes respect for and understanding of the mission and mandate of participating organizations. Each organization is encouraged to remain mindful of how to support the goals and objectives of other organizations while pursuing its own mandate.

Inclusive, Regular, and Frequent Face-to-Face, Peer-to-Peer Interaction

At JIATF-S, building respect for and understanding of the mission and mandate of participating organizations is accomplished, in part, through continuous interaction among LNOs and other staff. All JIATF-S staff are located in the task force's headquarters. Workspaces are arranged so that staff see each other working and are constantly exposed to each participating organization's specific issues of concern.

LNOs are fully embedded in the task force staff and command structure, so there is always something for them to do, especially as the flow of drug traffic in the JIATF-S AO is essentially unceasing. JIATF-S's constant operation creates a "live battle lab," in which relationships and structures can grow and be tested and techniques can be refined. Successful operations are constant reminders to all involved of the benefits of participation.

"Man-in-the-Loop" Command, Control, Communications, and Computers

JIATF-S coordinates and integrates a host of JIIM networks, systems, and capabilities. These include "agency-specific databases and networks, assets and forces contributed by partner nations, and partner-nation forces or assets that JIATF-S supports."[16] Rather than trying to force broad access into these systems, JIATF-S operates in a way that respects JIIM partners' accesses and controls. For example, CIA

---

[15] Munsing and Lamb, 2011, p. 50.

[16] Munsing and Lamb, 2011, p. 50.

databases are accessible only to LNOs from that agency, and only the Colombian LNO has the authority and communications equipment needed to control Colombian assets working with JIATF-S.

To protect proprietary systems and ensure appropriate controls, JIATF-S employs "man-in-the-loop" command, control, communications, and computers (C4). Networks and command and control (C2) systems are not directly integrated and made available to the entire staff. Instead, participating organizations use their own proprietary C4 resources, sharing permitted information—including invaluable contextual information.

A common example of this arrangement in action is an intelligence agency's production of "tear line" information. Using his or her own agency computer system, an LNO from a participating intelligence agency might see detailed information about a person of interest in a specific JIATF-S case. But that information might also be accompanied by highly sensitive information about intelligence sources and methods. In this situation, the LNO might share with the broader group the information that is "above the [tear] line"—e.g., operational details about the person of interest and his or her habits—while omitting sensitive information that cannot be shared.

On the JIATF-S joint interagency intelligence operations center floor, IC LNOs sit next to each other. Collocating LNOs from the IC, while at the same time giving each LNO access to his or her own agency systems, means that, through conversation and context, LNOs can share information while also maintaining necessary privacy.

This "man-in-the-loop" C4 arrangement is certainly more cumbersome and labor-intensive than one in which all C4 systems are fully integrated—intelligence fusion at JIATF-S can involve at least 22 databases.[17] However, participating organizations are unlikely to agree to completely integrate sensitive systems. Indeed, this sometimes cumbersome "man-in-the-loop" C4 arrangement is the only way to move information from one intelligence stovepipe to another while protecting the needs and priorities of both the originating source agency and the JIATF-S operational context.

---

[17] Munsing and Lamb, 2011, p. 48.

A Carefully Monitored System of Limited Disclosure and "Tear Lines"

Many factors impact whether and how information can be shared between and among agencies. In addition to common rules for handling and transmitting classified information, there are also requirements specific to different statutory authorities and to LESI. JIATF-S does not just accommodate these requirements—it embraces them. The aforementioned commitments to protecting participating organization equities and employing a "man-in-the-loop" C4 arrangement are, on the intelligence side of JIATF-S operations, supplemented with a carefully monitored system of limited disclosure and the aforementioned "tear lines." Time and again, JIATF-S demonstrates that it can respect equities while getting the right information to the right people.

Lessons Learned

The activities and conditions critical to JIATF-S success offer five lessons relevant to JIIM integration for Army tactical OCO. We expand on each lesson learned below.

Understanding and Serving Each Participating Organization's Equities Are Crucial

JIATF-S owes much of its success to the continued cooperation of its participating organizations. Without their intelligence, forces, assets, and other support, JIATF-S would be less capable and less effective. To encourage the continued cooperation of these participating organizations, JIATF-S continuously strives to understand and respect their equities. This entails involving participating organizations in decision-making and priority setting and protecting their needs for privacy.

Relationship-Building Takes Time

To successfully deploy tactical OCO, the Army must be able to build trust and operate with JIIM partners. JIATF-S was neither immediately successful in its mission nor immediately highly integrated with other organizations. Indeed, there were many false starts over a period of decades. And, even when the right conditions were in place, it took time to establish the organizational culture and traditions that enable JIATF-S's success. Relationships—both personal and institutional—matured over the course of years, not overnight.

To build a relationship with a potential participating organization, JIATF-S takes the first step of sending an LNO to that potential partner even before the organization has agreed to reciprocate. This is a "give to get" model. Initially, the LNOs sent to JIATF-S by participating organizations were not always agency superstars. However, trust has been developed and institutional buy-in has strengthened, and now the LNOs sent to JIATF-S by both U.S. agencies and partner nations are almost universally high performers. Today, a tour at JIATF-S is considered "an attractive stepping stone for careers in either law enforcement or interagency operations."[18] A JIATF-S tour is also a strong "ticket punch" for international LNOs. Many "return home to promotions and assignments of greater responsibility."[19]

A High Tempo of Operations Builds Cohesion

Operational commanders and cyber operators will need to work closely together with similar vocabularies and trust to perform OCO. A high tempo of operations can help form those conditions. JIATF-S's high tempo of operations affords several benefits in terms of building cohesion. First, relationships are forged and tested in the crucible of operations. LNOs and other staff must work together and smooth out kinks in actual operational contexts, where trust must be earned quickly and teamwork is essential. Second, there are plenty of opportunities to demonstrate success in the shared goal of combating illicit trafficking. Each participating organization sees the positive effects of cooperation with every interception and arrest. Finally, the pace of operations allows for "turn-taking." JIATF-S pursues so many cases that each participating organization sees its objectives advanced frequently enough to value participating in JIATF-S.

---

[18] Munsing and Lamb, 2011, p. 61.

[19] Munsing and Lamb, 2011, p. 62.

Collocation Increases Mutual Understanding Among Participating Organizations

Collocation of staff is critical to JIATF-S success. It facilitates respect for and understanding of the mission and mandate of participating organizations. All JIATF-S staff are in the task force's headquarters, and workspaces are arranged so that staff see each other working and are constantly being exposed to the specific issues of concern to particular participating organizations.

Even in an age of virtual communication, "there is no substitute for physical proximity and personal interaction" when it comes to creating opportunities to understand nonverbal cues, form bonds, and build a community.[20] And at JIATF-S, where turnover is relatively high, "participants agree there is no real substitute for collocation given the collaboration requirements of its core activity set."[21]

Information-Sharing Procedures and Rules Must Be Accommodated

Various agencies will be involved in tactical OCO and thus information sharing and rules will be vital to success. JIATF-S coordinates and integrates a host of JIIM networks, systems, and capabilities. Rather than trying to force broad access to these systems, JIATF-S operates in a way that respects the fact that many of these systems can only be accessed or controlled by appropriate JIIM staff. To protect proprietary systems and ensure appropriate controls, JIATF-S employs "man-in-the-loop" C4, in which participating organizations use their own proprietary C4 resources to share permitted information. On the intelligence side of JIATF-S operations, "man-in-the-loop" C4 is supplemented with a carefully monitored system of limited disclosure and the aforementioned "tear lines."

---

[20] Munsing and Lamb, 2011, p. 48.

[21] Munsing and Lamb, 2011, p. 48.

Chapter Summary

JIATF-S is a multiservice, multiagency task force based at Naval Air Station Key West in Key West, Florida. JIATF-S operations are driven by actionable intelligence that flows into the task force. The close relationship between intelligence partners and operators makes this a case study relevant to tactical cyber operations, which also require a close relationship between intelligence partners and operators. The activities and conditions critical to JIATF-S success offer five lessons, as shown in Table 2.1 below. Shared goals can be added to this list as well.

The strength of JIATF-S is the ability to mix and match capabilities and authorities to optimize the operational effectiveness of available assets. The Army should take note of these abilities, as they likely will be valuable for tactical cyber operations as such operations mature.

Table 2.1
Lessons Learned in Relationship to Tactical Cyber Operations

Lesson	Relevance to Tactical OCO
Understanding and serving each participating organization's equities are crucial.	Cyber/intel gain-loss considerations will be continuous.
Relationship-building takes time.	The Army must be able to build trust and operate with JIIM partners.
A high tempo of operations builds cohesion.	Operational commanders and cyber operators will need to work closely together with similar vocabularies and trust.
Collocation increases mutual understanding among participating organizations.	Commanders and cyber operators will need to work closely together, perhaps in close physical proximity to each other.
The information-sharing procedures and rules of participating organizations must be accommodated.	Various agencies could be involved in tactical OCO and thus information sharing and rules will be vital to success.

CHAPTER THREE

Case Study Two: U.S. Marine Corps Tactical SIGINT

To conduct and support OCO at all echelons, including tactical echelons, the Army will need to earn the trust of the IC and the cooperation of law-enforcement agencies and other partners that might not initially be comfortable with the concept of OCO at tactical levels.

In 2002, the USMC became the first service to receive the resources and authority necessary to access the nation's SIGINT databases quickly and efficiently while in theater. The USMC "earned" this streamlined access in increments from the NSA, which controls the SIGINT databases, through a combination of activities, including building and sustaining trust with the agency and demonstrating the value of the access it was requesting. This chapter examines how the USMC went about the difficult task of converting skepticism into cooperation.

An Introduction to SIGINT

The NSA is charged with the mission of collecting, processing, and disseminating intelligence information "from foreign signals for intelligence and counterintelligence purposes and to support military operations."[1] SIGINT—"intelligence derived from electronic signals and systems used by foreign targets, such as communications systems,

---

[1] NSA, "Mission," web page, April 15, 2011.

radars, and weapons systems"[2]—is one of the types of intelligence that the NSA collects, processes, and disseminates.

The NSA's SIGINT databases contain information of immeasurable value not only to strategists and analysts but also to combat forces.[3] For many years, however, military forces in theater had no quick or efficient way to access this vital information.

Today, all of the services enjoy streamlined access to the SIGINT databases, but the USMC paved the way. In 2002, during Operation Enduring Freedom, the USMC became the first service to receive the resources and authority necessary to access the SIGINT databases quickly and efficiently while in theater (see an example of in-theater access in Figure 3.1). This streamlined access made it possible for SIGINT Marines to provide previously unimagined support to Marines in combat. This streamlined access also made it possible for the USMC to make more-valuable contributions to the national SIGINT enterprise than ever before.

How the USMC Obtained SIGINT Access in Theater

It is no accident that the USMC was the first service to obtain streamlined access to the SIGINT databases. We identified nine USMC SIGINT activities that were instrumental in convincing the initially skeptical NSA to grant the necessary resources and authority.

Forging a Long-Term Working Relationship

The USMC SIGINT community's relationship with the NSA is a longstanding one. For decades, Marines (along with personnel from the other services) have spent time at the NSA's headquarters at Fort Meade in Anne Arundel County, Maryland, participating in training, detached to the NSA, or serving in formations stationed at Fort Meade

---

[2]   NSA, "Signals Intelligence," web page, March 2, 2015.

[3]   NSA, "The National Sigint Operations Center," *Cryptologic Spectrum*, Vol. 9, No. 3, Summer 1979, pp. 4–15.

in support of the NSA's mission. One such formation is the Marine Cryptologic Support Battalion, which trains and deploys Marines to carry out SIGINT and SIGINT-related missions.[4]

The USMC has also maintained a liaison office at the NSA since the 1990s. The LNOs who staff the office have helped develop and maintain a positive relationship between USMC SIGINT and the NSA. Since the beginning, they were also closely involved in doing whatever they could to get SIGINT Marines the information they needed as quickly as was possible at the time.

Thus, at the beginning of the 21st century, the USMC was already part of the SIGINT family. Indeed, SIGINT Marines were

Figure 3.1
A Marine Sets Up a Tactical SIGINT Collection System

SOURCE: U.S. Marine Corps Concepts and Programs, "Tactical Signals Intelligence (SIGINT) Collection System (TSCS)," web page, undated.
RAND RR1600-3.1

---

[4] U.S. Marine Corps, "Marine Cryptologic Support Battalion Intelligence Department," undated.

already "card-carrying members of the union," as one USMC civilian put it. They were known to and accepted by the NSA and the broader SIGINT enterprise, both as a group and, often, as individuals.

Knowing What Is Possible

SIGINT Marines were regular visitors to Fort Meade, and many had deployed as part of NSA forward detachments. They had worked with the latest gear, and they knew what it could do. Thus the USMC had a good idea of what might be possible when it came to using SIGINT on the battlefield. One of many examples of ideas for USMC tactical SIGINT was the ability to quickly push previously needed intelligence "down to the last tactical mile."[5] Another was rapidly targeting adversaries using geolocation information from insurgents' wireless devices.[6]

Seizing an Opportunity

Early on in Operation Enduring Freedom, the "perfect storm" for requesting streamlined access to the SIGINT databases arose, bringing together two compelling arguments: technology and circumstance. Early deployments of Marines to Afghanistan coincided with the first deployment of new communications systems that dramatically increased the bandwidth available on the battlefield. SIGINT Marines (who operated alongside maneuver forces) believed that the bandwidth afforded by these new systems would make streamlined access to the SIGINT databases technologically possible.

Meanwhile, on the ground, Marines, other U.S. troops, and coalition forces were being put in harm's way and sustaining casualties. SIGINT Marines had a compelling argument for doing whatever they

---

[5]   Robert K. Ackerman, "Joint Approach Defines Marine Corps Intelligence," *Signal*, April 2004.

[6]   Kristin Quinn, "C4ISR Journal Announces Award Winners," *DefenseNews*, October 15, 2010.

could to better support these forces, and for encouraging the NSA to do the same.[7]

Leveraging Individual Relationships
When the USMC first asked the NSA for the resources and authorities necessary to quickly and efficiently access the SIGINT databases from the battlefield, the NSA said no. The agency was simply not inclined to grant this streamlined access to young, unknown men with guns. However, many SIGINT Marines had not only spent time at Fort Meade, but were well known to and respected by NSA personnel. When these individuals themselves asked for the necessary resources and authorities, they often got them, due to these personal relationships of trust.

Accepting Conditions Unconditionally
In requesting streamlined access to the SIGINT databases, the USMC agreed to abide by—and did indeed diligently adhere to—any and all constraints, rules, and oversight requirements imposed by the NSA. The USMC's willingness to accept any conditions to get a foot in the door made it hard for the NSA to say no, and the USMC's continued diligence made it hard for the NSA to change its initial "yes" to a "no" as time went on. By demonstrating "good citizenship" and respecting the NSA's conditions, the USMC continued to earn the trust of the NSA and began to pave the way for the relaxation of some of the initial constraints imposed by the agency.

Demonstrating Success
SIGINT Marines experienced early success in using USMC tactical SIGINT to positively and directly affect "the situation and the tactical stance" of combat forces.[8] One of many success stories is the role played by 2nd Radio Battalion, Task Force Belleau Wood, in stopping

---

[7] Some have speculated that the President was instrumental here by instructing the IC to increase cooperation with the services on counterterrorism issues. Cynthia Dion-Schwarz, personal communication with the author, April 4, 2016.

[8] Bryan J. Nygard, "Radio Battalion Helps ANGLICO Intercept Insurgents," June 6, 2011.

an improvised explosive device (IED) attack by insurgents in Afghanistan. "When Radio Battalion got out here, they opened our eyes as to where the Taliban were hiding," said Lance Cpl. Andrew J. Armstrong, a forward observer with Fire Control Team 5. "They're the Marine Corps' greatest asset out here right now. Those guys are money."[9] Successes helped the USMC continue to make a case for further relaxation of constraints and for the institutionalization of hitherto provisional or ad hoc access.

Smoothing the Way for Institutionalization

Diligent adherence to NSA rules and demonstrated success on the battlefield helped increase the NSA's comfort with USMC tactical SIGINT. But there was still the possibility of a crisis in confidence when SIGINT Marines who had personally requested streamlined access rotated out of theater. Having trusted SIGINT Marines train the second generation of SIGINT Marines helped establish both continuity and a legacy.

Giving Back

By the time USMC tactical SIGINT in theater became mature, SIGINT Marines were no longer just consumers of NSA resources: They were actively contributing to the national SIGINT enterprise in unprecedented ways. In addition to meeting their own operational requirements (thereby reducing the number of USMC requests for assistance from the NSA), they were both collecting and analyzing valuable SIGINT and pushing it up to the national SIGINT enterprise. Rather than just being "takers" and "consumers," SIGINT Marines had become "givers" and "contributors." This created a win-win situation for the USMC, the NSA, and the national SIGINT enterprise.

Maintaining a Liaison Office

During the evolution of USMC tactical SIGINT, much of the negotiating was done or facilitated by the USMC SIGINT liaison office at the NSA. This office—whose personnel describe themselves as aggressive

---

[9]   Nygard, 2011.

and innovative, but responsible—plays a number of roles in sustaining the positive relationship between USMC SIGINT and the NSA.

LNOs serve as ambassadors for both communities, ensuring that USMC interests and concerns are communicated clearly to the NSA, and vice versa. The office acts as a customer-service center for USMC operating forces. LNOs "translate" NSA policies and help Marines in the field understand what they have to do to get the data and tools they need while following the rules. The NSA is a large organization, so the office also plays the role of advocate for the USMC. For example, LNOs ensure that deploying Marines are placed on the correct NSA distribution lists, granted access to the right databases, equipped with the right tools, and trained and certified to use those tools.

Lessons Learned

The evolution of USMC tactical SIGINT offers five lessons regarding how the Army can earn the trust of the NSA and other IC, law-enforcement, and additional partners that might be skeptical of Army OCO at tactical levels, as listed in Table 3.1.

Table 3.1
Lessons Learned in Relationship to Tactical Cyber Operations

Lesson	Relationship to Tactical OCO
Preparation makes it possible to seize an opportunity to get a foot in the door.	
Ongoing operations can demonstrate success and trustworthiness.	To conduct and support OCO at all echelons, including tactical echelons, the Army will need to earn the trust of the IC and the cooperation of law-enforcement agencies and other partners.
Understanding and serving a partner's equities are crucial.	
Establishing a presence in the partner organization can be instrumental in success.	
Accepting conditions unconditionally makes it hard for a partner to say "no."	

Preparation Makes It Possible to Seize an Opportunity to Get a Foot in the Door

Operation Enduring Freedom brought together two compelling arguments—technology and circumstance—for requesting streamlined access to the SIGINT databases. But the USMC was also prepared to seize this opportunity: The USMC SIGINT community had a long-standing and positive relationship with the NSA, it was aware of what was possible, and it was able to leverage both working and individual relationships.

Ongoing Operations Can Demonstrate Success and Trustworthiness

Early success in using USMC tactical SIGINT to improve results on the battlefield helped the USMC continue to make a case for further relaxation of constraints and for the institutionalization of hitherto provisional or ad hoc access. Strict adherence to the initial constraints imposed by the NSA was a continual reminder to the agency that its trust in the USMC was not misplaced.

Understanding and Serving a Partner's Equities Are Crucial

By signaling its willingness to accept any and all initial conditions, the USMC adopted an opening negotiation position that clearly subordinated its goals and interests to those of the NSA. Continued "good citizenship," respect for NSA oversight, incremental requests for additional access, and the fact that SIGINT Marines were soon "giving back" rather than just taking helped the NSA see USMC tactical SIGINT—which could have been viewed as burdensome or unwise—as a net positive for the national SIGINT enterprise.

Establishing a Presence in the Partner Organization Can Be Instrumental in Success

It is no accident that the USMC was the first service to obtain access to the national SIGINT enterprise while in theater. At the beginning of the 21st century, SIGINT Marines were already known to and accepted by the NSA (both as a group and, often, as individuals), and the USMC had maintained a USMC SIGINT liaison office at the NSA for many years. This was an early, positive, and enduring presence at the NSA that set an example. Individual and working relationships developed between SIGINT Marines and NSA staff over time proved instrumental in convincing the NSA to take the first cautious steps toward granting SIGINT Marines streamlined access to the SIGINT databases.

Meanwhile, USMC SIGINT LNOs kept lines of communication open between the USMC and the NSA; ensured that deploying Marines had the access, tools, and training they needed; and helped Marines in the field understand and adhere to NSA policies.

Accepting Conditions Unconditionally Makes It Hard for a Partner to Say "No"

In requesting streamlined access to the SIGINT databases, the USMC agreed to abide the constraints, rules, and oversight requirements imposed by the NSA. The USMC's willingness to accept any conditions in order to get a foot in the door made it hard for the NSA to say no, and the USMC's continued diligence made it hard for the NSA to change its initial "yes" to a "no" as time went on. By demonstrating "good citizenship" and respecting the NSA's conditions, the USMC continued to earn the trust of the NSA and began to pave the way for the relaxation of some of the initial constraints imposed by the agency.

Chapter Summary

To conduct and support OCO at all echelons, including tactical echelons, the Army will need to earn the trust of the IC and the cooperation of law-enforcement agencies and other partners. The lessons described in this chapter and shown in Table 3.1 are all requirements toward earning that trust. In the face of great skepticism, the USMC became the first service to receive the resources and authority necessary to access the nation's SIGINT databases quickly and efficiently while in theater. This chapter examined how the USMC went about the difficult task of converting skepticism into cooperation.

CHAPTER FOUR

Case Study Three: The Use of Armed Drones

In the post-9/11 security environment, drone warfare has become increasingly important and prevalent. Its use has outpaced the development and codification of the laws and policies designed to govern how this technology is used on the battlefield. The same can be said of cyber warfare.

In pursuing tactical OCO, the Army has and/or is likely to encounter many of the challenges surrounding the use of armed drones, including legal and policy challenges; questions related to authorities, oversight, and transparency; and other contentious issues, such as "blowback," de-confliction, compliance with U.S. law, and collateral damage.

This chapter examines the still-evolving policies, laws, challenges, and debates surrounding the use of armed drones with an eye toward illuminating the challenges the Army is likely to face as it operates with existing authorities and prepares to operate within authorities it might gain in the future. This chapter is closely linked to our recommendation to respect constraints, since current authorities for tactical OCO are both murky and evolving. Until those authorities are clarified and devolved, they will remain deliberately granted by and managed at higher (e.g., strategic and operational) echelons. The Army should plan to coordinate with these higher echelons.

Why Compare Drones and Cyber?

Immediately after 9/11, it became apparent to the broader national security community that drones would be an important part of the fight against al Qaida, both in terms of using weaponized drones and also for less obviously kinetic tasks like ISR.

Like drone warfare, cyber warfare has become increasingly important and prevalent, especially in conducting operations against a range of adversaries, from nonstate threats like the Islamic State in Iraq and Syria (ISIS) to near-peer adversaries, such as Iran and North Korea. Threat planning impacts ISR, OPE, and the effects commanders can pursue against these adversaries. Increasingly, tactical offensive cyber operations are widely acknowledged as a necessary and effective tool in the U.S. military's arsenal,[1] and is likely to remain vital in the coming years.[2]

Both technologies have outpaced the development and codification of laws designed to govern how they are employed on the battlefield. Laws tend to evolve at a slow, deliberate pace, whereas technological innovation, including "all things cyber," occurs very rapidly.[3] The lag between technology and the development and codification of laws and policy was overcome with respect to drones, due in no small measure to the necessity of this technology as a counterterrorism and warfighting tool, but reconciling authorities between the military and the IC is still a challenge.

The debates surrounding armed drones and cyber warfare are occurring in a complex interagency environment that includes Congress, the IC, the NSA, the White House, and DoD, among others. Nevertheless, the use of both armed drones and cyber warfare continues to accelerate.

---

[1] Johnston and Sarbahi, 2016. Research by Johnston and Sarbahi argues that by enabling both intelligence collection through overhead surveillance and direct targeting of suspected terrorists, drones reduce militant violence by increasing the costs of militant activities and creating an incentive for militants to "lie low" to avoid being targeted.

[2] Johnston and Sarbahi, 2016.

[3] Jason Andress and Steve Winterfeld, *Cyber Warfare: Techniques, Tactics and Tools for Security Practitioners*, Waltham, Mass.: Syngress, 2011, p. 209.

In spite of these similarities, there are, of course, differences between the use of armed drones and cyber warfare. These differences are quite evident when one considers the characteristics of lethality and mission scope. Damage from armed drones is physical—often lethal—but it can be limited to a specific geographic area of operations. On the other hand, cyber warfare has the potential to inflict damage on a transnational scale if cyber systems are highly interconnected (e.g., through the Internet). Interconnectivity can result in OCO aimed at a specific target having unexpected and undesired consequences.[4]

The Use of Armed Drones in Operation Enduring Freedom

As noted earlier, the lag between drone technology and the development and codification of relevant laws and policy has not prevented or even slowed the use of drone warfare. Indeed, armed drones have become an essential tool in the fight against transnational terrorism. Drone strikes have been employed against a range of nonstate actors, including members of al-Shabaab in Somalia, al Qaida in the Arabian Peninsula in Yemen, and the Haqqani Network in Afghanistan and Pakistan, to name only a few.

The armed drone campaign began during President George W. Bush's administration, but, under President Barack Obama's administration, it has intensified. In his first four years in office, President Obama authorized 283 strikes in Pakistan alone—a six-fold increase over the total number of authorizations made by President Bush during his eight years in the White House.[5]

Applicable Laws
Relevant laws are complex and evolving. We elaborate as follows.

---

[4]   Mark M. Lowenthal, *Intelligence: From Secrets to Policy*, 5th ed., Los Angeles, Calif.: Sage, 2012.

[5]   Peter Bergan and Megan Braun, "Drone Is Obama's Weapon of Choice," CNN, September 5, 2012.

On September 30, 2011, Anwar al-Awlaki, an American-born al Qaida in the Arabian Peninsula senior operative and a high-value target, was killed by a Hellfire missile launched by a Predator drone. This strike "provided a stark, concrete case of a U.S. policy that authorizes death for terrorists, even when they're Americans," and it "reenergized" the ongoing national debate over "the legal and moral quandaries of a government deliberately killing a citizen."[6]

In the aftermath of the attack, some denounced the strike as a "targeted killing program [that] violates both U.S. and international law" and protested that al-Awlaki was a U.S. citizen targeted for death without his legal right to due process.[7] In June 2014, a federal court released a previously classified memo written by lawyers in the Department of Justice's Office of Legal Counsel. The memo stated that al-Awlaki's citizenship did not impose "constitutional limitations that would preclude the contemplated lethal action," thus clearing the way for a drone strike.[8] Other justifications included the fact that, at the time the memo was written, al-Awlaki had "operational and leadership roles" with al Qaida and continued to "plot attacks intended to kill Americans."[9]

Executive Order 12333. Leaving aside the question of al-Awlaki's U.S. citizenship, it is important to note that the use of assassination as a tool of U.S. policy is outlawed by Executive Order (EO) 12333. Signed in 1981 by President Ronald Reagan, EO 12333 informs the legality of a range of issues, including information-collection techniques, human experimentation, and the use of assassination.

Section 2.11, *Prohibition on Assassination*, pertains to the use of armed drones to conduct counterterrorist strikes. The section stipulates that "no person employed by or acting on behalf of the United States

---

[6]   Michael Martinez, "U.S. Drone Killing of American al-Awlaki Prompts Legal, Moral Debate," CNN, September 30, 2011.

[7]   Martinez, 2011.

[8]   Greg Miller, "Legal Memo Backing Drone Strike That Killed American Anwar al-Awlaki Is Released," *Washington Post*, June 23, 2014.

[9]   Miller, 2014.

Government shall engage in, or conspire to engage in, assassination." However, EO 12333 is not the only document relevant to this case.

The 2001 Authorization for the Use of Military Force. The 2001 Authorization for the Use of Military Force, passed by Congress shortly after the attacks on 9/11, grants the President the power to employ "all necessary and appropriate force" to pursue those responsible for the attacks.[10]

The U.S. Constitution. Article II of the U.S. Constitution confers upon the President the powers of commander in chief and executor of the nation's laws.[11] The targeting of al-Awlaki falls within the "national self-defense" framework derived from the President's constitutional security powers.

The Charter of the United Nations. Article 51 of the Charter of the United Nations states that "nothing in the present Charter shall impair the inherent right of individual or collective self-defence if an armed attack occurs against a member of the United Nations, until the Security Council has taken measures necessary to maintain international peace and security." The White House has maintained that the U.S. right to self-defense

> may include the targeted killing of persons such as high-level al-Qaeda leaders who are planning attacks, both in and out of declared theaters of war. The administration's posture includes the prerogative to unilaterally pursue targets in states without prior consent if that country is unwilling or unable to deal effectively with the threat.[12]

Oversight

Another contentious legal aspect of the armed drone campaign is oversight. The two pieces of U.S. Code in question are Title 10 and Title 50. Title 10 "gives the Secretary of Defense all 'authority, direc-

---

[10]   Pub L. 107-40, 2001.

[11]   U.S. Constitution, Article II, §§ 2–3.

[12]   Jonathan Masters, "Targeted Killings," Council on Foreign Relations, February 8, 2013.

tion and control' over DoD, including all subordinate agencies and commands."[13] Title 50 "establishes, defines, and delineates authorities within the IC."[14]

Because drone attacks can take place under the auspices of either Joint Special Operations Command or the CIA, either Title 10 or Title 50 can apply. However, the former are considered clandestine operations, while the latter are considered covert.[15] When a strike is deemed to fall under Title 10 authorities, the Senate Armed Services Committee and the House Armed Services Committee have oversight. When a strike is deemed to fall under Title 50 authorities, the Senate Select Committee on Intelligence and the House Permanent Select Committee on Intelligence have oversight.[16] Members of the Senate intelligence committees have been granted access to Department of Justice memos justifying the use of drones, and members of both the House and Senate intelligence committees have been allowed to review individual completed strikes as well as "a sampling of the intelligence buttressing each strike."[17]

---

[13] Wall, 2011.

[14] Wall, 2011.

[15] DoD defines a clandestine operation as an "operation sponsored or conducted by governmental departments or agencies in such a way as to assure secrecy or concealment" (DoD, *Dictionary of Military and Associated Terms*, JP 1-02, November 8, 2010 [as amended through February 15, 2016], p. 33). A clandestine operation differs from a covert operation in that emphasis is placed on concealment of the operation rather than on the identity of the sponsor. In special operations, an activity may be both covert and clandestine and may focus equally on operational considerations and intelligence related activities. DoD defines a covert operation as "an operation that is so planned and executed to conceal the identity of or permit plausible denial by the sponsor" (DoD, 2016). On this distinction, see Chad C. Serena, *It Takes More Than a Network: The Iraqi Insurgency and Organizational Adaptation*, Stanford, Calif.: Stanford University Press, 2014, p. 150.

[16] Wall, 2011.

[17] Dylan Matthews, "Everything You Need to Know About the Drone Debate, in One FAQ," *Washington Post*, March 8, 2013; see also Mark Mazzetti and Matt Apuzzo, "Deep Support in Washington for C.I.A.'s Drone Missions," *New York Times*, April 25, 2015.

General Considerations Related to State Conduct in Cyberspace

According to the International Strategy for Cyberspace released by the White House in May 2011, "long-standing international norms guiding state behavior—in times of peace and conflict—also apply in cyberspace."[18] Essentially, this means that *jus in bello* rules apply to OCO. Therefore, the principles of necessity and proportionality limit the use of force in self-defense and regulate what constitutes a lawful response under the circumstances.[19] Quoting a "senior American official," a *New York Times* article likened the power of cyber weapons to those of nuclear weapons and concluded that there are "very, very few instances" in which cyber operations would be decided at any level below the President.[20] As of June 2013, the National Security Council must officially approve any cyber effect.[21]

Obama's attempt in May 2013 to clarify drone policy seems to suggest that drone operations will be shifted entirely from the CIA to DoD.[22] Part of this debate revolves around the traditional responsibility of the IC, which has taken on more of a paramilitary role in the post-9/11 environment. It is not outside of the realm of possibility that the President will rely on Title 50 covert-action authority for future potential cyber actions,[23] thus making deconfliction a challenge for Title 10–authorized forces.

---

[18]   White House, *International Strategy for Cyberspace: Prosperity*, Security and Openness in a Networked World, Washington, D.C., May 2011.

[19]   Michael N. Schmitt, "International Law in Cyberspace: The Koh Speech and Tallinn Manual Juxtaposed," *Harvard International Law Journal*, Vol. 54, December 2012.

[20]   David E. Sanger and Thom Shanker, "Broad Powers Seen for Obama in Cyberstrikes," *New York Times*, February 3, 2013.

[21]   Fryer-Biggs, 2013.

[22]   Jeremy Herb, "Fewer Drone Strikes Likely the Result of New Obama Policy, Analysts Say," *The Hill*, May 27, 2013.

[23]   For more on covert action, see Gregory Treverton, *Covert Action: The Limits of Intervention in the Postwar World*, New York: Basic Books, 1987; and Stephen Dycuss, *National Security Law*, 3rd ed., New York: Aspen, 2002.

The authorities question is inextricably linked to several other ancillary issues, including the fear of "blowback" from the use of OCO, the difficulty of deconfliction, challenges related to attribution, and collateral damage and the concept of proportionality, among others.

Blowback. *Blowback* refers to the unintended consequences of a covert operation that are suffered by the civilian population of the government in charge of that operation. As Mark Lowenthal states, "not all covert actions remain covert."[24] One potential example of blowback is other countries or nonstate actors justifying cyber attacks against the United States on the basis of the fact that the U.S. government employs cyber warfare.[25] This example is not at all far-fetched. In early 2013, the Chinese government acknowledged contemplating using drone strikes to target a high-level drug trafficker in Myanmar, noting that the government in Naypyidaw was either unwilling or unable to suppress the threat posed by the trafficker. The Chinese government used language similar to that used by the Obama administration as the rationale for the U.S. drone program.[26] (It is important that blowback not be confused with collateral damage, which is governed by the law of armed conflict.)[27]

Although it is mostly true that the United States is the only country using drones on a regular basis, evidence strongly suggests that adversaries are already using OCO at the tactical level. Therefore, U.S. actions would not be precedent-setting inasmuch as they would be responsive. For example, in the 2008 Russia-Georgia conflict, OCO were integrated with traditional operations to enhance overall oper-

---

[24] Lowenthal, 2012, p. 167.

[25] Joseph Menn, "Special Report: U.S. Cyberwar Strategy Stokes Fear of Blowback," *Reuters*, May 10, 2013.

[26] J. Dana Stutser, "China Now Considering Drone Strikes in Its Drug War," *Foreign Policy*, February 19, 2013; Jane Perlez, "Chinese Plan to Kill Drug Lord with Drone Highlights Military Advances," *New York Times*, February 20, 2013.

[27] A good discussion of cyber collateral damage can be found in Richard Clarke and Robert K. Knake, *Cyber War*, New York: Harper Collins, 2010, pp. 202–206.

ational effectiveness.[28] Similar or more-advanced operations could be taking place today in the ongoing conflict between Russia and Ukraine, where Russian troops are playing a major role in supporting rebel forces.

Deconfliction. Deconfliction is an information- and intelligence-sharing process used to determine whether multiple agencies are targeting the same individual or organization. It notifies agencies of their shared interest in the case and supplies contact information in an attempt to both minimize conflicts between agencies and maximize the effectiveness of the investigation or operation.

Attribution. Identifying the perpetrator of a cyber attack can be a challenge, but it is also critical to making decisions about the appropriate response. The United States faces a wide range of potential cyber attackers: cyber terrorists, cyber spies, cyber thieves, cyber hacktivists, and quasistate agents known as *cyber warriors*.[29] Responding to a cyber attack requires knowing which individual, state, or organization was behind the attack. Attribution can be complicated by a host of analytical shortcomings, such as those evident in prior intelligence failures, including the flawed estimate of Iraq's weapons of mass destruction program.[30] As previously noted, the sheer number of possible adversaries, from Eastern European hackers to Iranian state-sponsored cyber specialists, makes immediate attribution more difficult.

Proportionality. To ensure compliance with international law, any response to a cyber attack must be consonant with the principles of proportionality. The elimination of signature strikes as part of the armed drone campaign seems to address this issue—between 258 and 307 civilians have been killed in Pakistan alone—and answers critics who claim that drone attacks have become an extremely useful recruit-

---

[28] David Hollis, "Cyberwar Case Study: Georgia 2008," *Small Wars Journal*, January 6, 2011.

[29] Eric A. Fischer, Edward C. Liu, John Rollins, and Catherine A. Theohary, *The 2013 Cybersecurity Executive Order: Overview and Considerations for Congress*, Washington, D.C.: Congressional Research Service Report, March 1, 2013.

[30] Marshall Curtis Erwin, *Intelligence Issues for Congress*, Washington, D.C.: Congressional Research Service Report, April 23, 2013.

ing tool for militants.[31] Those who worry about the proportionality of cyber attacks frequently cite the nightmare scenario of a U.S. cyber attack mistakenly causing a power outage at a hospital outside the United States and the resulting public relations fiasco that would ensue for the United States.

Consensus About Implied Authorities to Use Tactical Cyber Operations Is Lacking

According to a TRADOC white paper, "Enabling Operations in Cyberspace Through Institutional and Operational Unity of Effort," defensive cyberspace operations (DCO), whether they fall under Title 10 or Title 50, must include the ability to conduct reconnaissance of adversary networks and hunt operations inside and outside the LandWarNet.[32] Hunting, in this case, is defined as "the act of searching for; seeking; endeavoring to obtain, or find something, good or bad, in cyberspace through the enterprise, regional, and local levels."[33] But, as with cyber exploitation, use of these reconnaissance activities has led to concerns over violating U.S. domestic law, including EO 12333, despite current Army regulations in place to assuage concerns about such violations.[34] But a June 2015 report from DoD on the Law of War acknowledges that reconnaissance, to include mapping a network, is a lawful cyber operation in wartime.[35] Moreover, most states would regard mapping networks as falling under applicable international law in peacetime.[36]

---

[31] Herb, 2013. Signature strikes are based on pattern-of-life analysis. For example, the exact identity of a target might be unknown, but his or her behavior fits the pattern of a terrorist. See Daniel Byman, "Why Drones Work: The Case for Washington's Weapon of Choice," *Foreign Affairs*, Vol. 92, No. 4, July/August 2013, p. 36.

[32] TRADOC, "Enabling Operations in Cyberspace Through Institutional and Operational Unity of Effort White Paper," July 9, 2013, pp. 8–10.

[33] U.S. Army Cyber Command, "LandCyber White Paper: 2018–2030," Ft. Meade, Md., September 9, 2013.

[34] U.S. Army Cyber Command, 2013.

[35] DoD, *Department of Defense Law of War Manual*, Washington, D.C.: Office of General Counsel, Department of Defense, June 2015b, p. 995.

[36] Greg Austin, "The Pentagon's Law of War for Cyberspace," *Diplomat*, December 22, 2015.

The constitutional rights of U.S. Persons (USPs) require a delicate balance between protecting individual liberties on the one hand and, on the other, the interest of the United States government in protecting and defending its citizens. When the interests of the government outweigh a USP's right to privacy, *the U.S. government can collect intelligence on that USP.*[37] Indeed, USP information may be intentionally collected if it is necessary for the maintenance of national security or for the success of a military mission, including those described in Army Regulation (AR) 381-10.

AR 381-10 discusses "U.S. Army Intelligence Activities" and describes when and how the U.S. government can collect intelligence on a USP.[38] It is important to note that any person, association, or corporation outside of the United States is presumed to be a non-USP unless specific information to the contrary is obtained.[39] Until there is evidence proving otherwise, even people who strongly appear to be USPs can be treated as non-USPs.

In the cyber domain, these provisions and their implementation are less clear cut. In cyberspace, intelligence activities are typically focused, at least initially, more on individuals and less on, for example, their Internet Protocol (IP) addresses, URLs, and e-mail addresses. Additionally, there is a distinction between acquiring, retaining, and processing and analyzing. If the activity simply involves collecting and reporting information without any analysis or without trying to determine more about the information and the addresses, then the issue of whether an activity is focused on a USP is irrelevant. However, if the objective is to analyze the information, AR 381-10 requires a "reasonable and diligent inquiry" to determine whether the IP address or e-mail address is associated with a USP. Because AR 381-10 does not define "reasonable and diligent inquiry," the most appropriate next step

---

[37] Office of the Staff Judge Advocate, USAICoE and Ft. Huachuca, Intelligence Law & Instructor Division, "Intelligence Oversight," HUMINT Legal Principles, October 3, 2006.

[38] Specifically, Procedures Two, Three, and Four apply only when collecting on a USP. These procedures are titled "Collecting on US Persons," "Retaining US Person Information," and "Disseminating US Person Information," respectively.

[39] Office of the Staff Judge Advocate, 2006.

would be to ask a staff Judge Advocate General (or other appropriate legal advisor/counsel) for a legal review.

Still, it is important to note that for each intelligence discipline, EO 12333 defines interagency coordination requirements for operations. It does not confer any intelligence authorities on the Army but delegates those authorities to the "Intelligence Components Utilized by the Secretary of Defense." In EO 12333 Section 1.12(b)(8), the NSA is tasked with "executing the responsibilities of the Secretary of Defense as executive agent for the communications security of the United States Government."[40] This aggregation of authority and responsibility under presidential directive gives the NSA unique power and leverage in U.S. government and DoD cyberspace operations.

Findings, Policy Implications, and Recommendations

Opinions differ within the national security IC, DoD, and the Army itself over which cyber authorities exist and exactly how they should be interpreted. As of today, the tactical commander is limited to providing basic defensive measures to protect his or her cyber assets (defending a brigade's own network is a difficult job in and of itself). It is still unclear which types of OCO are authorized at the tactical level; a detailed set of guidelines needs to be established.

Cultivating an offensive cyber capability is one of the three critical pillars of "the New Triad" (special operations forces, unmanned vehicles, and cyber capabilities).[41] Although OCO do not currently exist at the tactical level—and never will, according to some—the future needs of the mission commander will likely dictate what is eventually allowed as policy matures.

Most of the lessons from case studies one and two concern the issue of organizational adaptation, whereas case study three's are more relevant to tactical employability. However, the case of armed drones

---

[40] National Archives, Federal Register, Executive Order 12333, "United States Intelligence Activities," December 4, 1981.

[41] James Stavridis, "The New Triad," *Foreign Policy*, June 20, 2013.

does offer lessons relevant to organization. First, in spite of the lack of clear lines of jurisdiction and responsibility, the operational necessity of the mission resulted in multiple high-level authorizations. To disrupt the al Qaida network and its regional affiliates across the world, the United States went on the offensive and learned by doing.

Second, to the extent that drones have been effective, there is a need to recognize the importance of working with local partners. This can only be done by liaising and having a forward presence, however limited, where a robust intelligence apparatus on the ground can provide context to an otherwise fluid situation and potentially mitigate collateral damage.

Chapter Summary

The United States' use of armed drones during Operation Enduring Freedom offers a single overarching lesson regarding what the Army will have to address if it hopes to be able to employ OCO at the tactical level: For any capability developed, concerns regarding deconfliction, attribution, and proportionality will have to be addressed. The military, the IC, and U.S. policymakers have managed to mutually respect agreed-upon constraints. To date, the required congressional oversight has been respected in attempt to maintain transparency with Congress— both to earn much-needed support and to avoid political consequences. The United States's use of armed drones during Operation Enduring Freedom offers an overarching lesson regarding what the Army will have to address if it hopes to be able to employ OCO at the tactical level.

CHAPTER FIVE

An Approach to Army Tactical OCO: Tethering

If the evolution of armed drone policy and practice is any indication, most OCO will, in the immediate future, continue to be authorized only at the highest echelons, but they will still occur—at some echelon, via joint and interagency partnerships—as dictated by the mission. Commanders at progressively lower levels of command will "need" to conduct tactical cyber operations, including OCO.[1] The Army needs novel ways to coordinate among tactical and strategic agencies and organizations to achieve cyber effects locally.

Although cyber operational capability at tactical levels is not a new concept, cyber operational expertise in the Army remains a scarce resource. This challenge is most apparent at tactical levels, where there are no dedicated, organic capabilities for OCO. As the Army develops concepts, doctrine, and capabilities to support OCO at tactical levels, it must bear this in mind. A unit or organization that enables a tight coupling between rear and forward echelons—as described in

---

[1] When considering the panoply of challenges facing the Army in the near- to middle-future, one need look no further than the complex and volatile situation unfolding in Syria today. Syrian regular army units are backed by an international terrorist organization (Hizballah) and receive training and equipment from Iran's Revolutionary Guards to fight against a patchwork of Syrian rebels, including previously al Qaida–linked Jabhat al-Fateh al-Sham and other Sunni insurgents. Moreover, a shadowy organization calling itself the Syrian Electronic Army has claimed responsibility for numerous cyber attacks against Western news outlets, including the Associated Press.

this chapter—could mitigate previously discussed concerns related to blowback and collateral damage.[2]

The Emerging Opportunity

There is broad agreement that military forces at tactical levels are permitted and should be required to routinely conduct basic DCO (e.g., cybersecurity or information assurance tasks, such as patching and monitoring). However, the services could well find themselves operating in a more permissive environment, one that allows more aggressive measures to defend and achieve the mission, including tactical OCO.

Uncertainty about which kinds of tactical OCO are allowed today—let alone in the future—suggests that authorities for these operations will remain deliberately granted and managed at higher (e.g., strategic and operational) echelons, at least in the near term. Nonetheless, Army strategists and planners (and in the U.S. military more broadly) are thinking about possible changes in the authorities that could afford them more flexibility at tactical levels.

For example, at the Armed Forces Communications and Electronics Association TechNet Augusta 2014 conference, a panel of chief warrant officers discussed "the possibility of cyber attacks being launched by brigade combat teams." CW4 Paul Gross of the Cyber Center of Excellence in Fort Gordon, Georgia, "told the audience he wants to see offensive cyber operations conducted at the lowest possible level."[3] He contended that "the threat's already huge, and as the capabilities that our adversaries have grow, we're going to need more people

---

[2]   A major issue with OCO is the strategic corporal problem, where "the corporal's rifle can fire around the globe and hit any number of unknown targets" (Andrew Metcalf and Christopher Barber, "Tactical Cyber: How to Move Forward," *Small Wars Journal*, September 14, 2014). Needless to say, there would be serious diplomatic ramifications if a cyber effect violates the neutrality of or interferes with the sovereignty of other countries. Laws and authorities sometimes perceived as "limiting" or "constraining" are meant to guard against such fallout.

[3]   George I. Seffers, "Blog: Future Army May Need Offensive Cyber Operations at the Tactical Edge," *Signal*, September 9, 2014.

to conduct those operations."[4] Pushing OCO to tactical levels, Gross suggested, "will provide commanders a wider range of options."

If and when the needed authorities are clarified and/or available, OCO at tactical levels will be acceptable. In the interim, while the authority to conduct OCO rests at higher echelons, one approach to enable OCO at tactical levels comes from an unlikely source: Hollywood.

Learning from *Aliens*: Remotely Supported Cyber Operators

In James Cameron's 1986 film *Aliens*, a squad of "U.S. Colonial Marines" advances on an abandoned mining facility. When the large secure door to the facility cannot be opened, the squad sergeant summons PFC William Hudson, a combat technician. He produces a pack of tools, opens the console to the door, and attaches alligator clips to a device he carries. Hudson does a few more things off camera, and the door opens, possibly with the support of someone more technically sophisticated back on the mother ship.

In this vignette, a specially trained marine performs a set of activities with specialized equipment, likely receiving support from what would be analogous to today's reachback facilities. This could be a model for Army offensive tactical cyber operations: Remotely supported cyber operators (RSCOs) could perform activities at tactical levels with reachback support. Indeed, in describing a "way ahead for tactical cyber," U.S. Army Cyber Commander LTG Edward C. Cardon suggested that "small cyberteams could be attached to brigades or lower level units. These teams would be 'tethered' back to national-level agencies for the sake of obtaining authorization to act."[5]

---

[4]   Seffers, 2014.

[5]   Gould, 2014.

Discussion on Practical Considerations

A major challenge observed based on the experiences with the defensive side of cyber operations is the difficulty in specifying, building, and maintaining a "fly-away" kit. Both the Air Force and Army have experienced challenges with regard to establishing a process and putting in place personnel for the appropriate type of units to ensure all the defensive cyber "fly-away" kits are up-to-date and ready for operation. A new structure and/or organizational element may need to be developed, along the lines of the proposed "Cyber Support Teams," whose sole focus would be on the maintenance, updates, calibration, and readiness of the cyber platform, just as an Air Force crew ensures an airframe is fully maintained, up-to-date, and ready to fly and fight. This could be a challenge on the offensive side, particularly given the need to ensure a potentially lethal weapon has been reviewed by the appropriate organizations.[6]

"Tethered" Tactical OCO

Many cyberspace operations can be accomplished remotely—virtually anywhere and by anyone with the proper authorities, training, equipment, and relationships with JIIM partners. What the Army provides is the connection and coordination necessary to ensure that these remote operations are available to support commanders on the ground. This connection and coordination should not be trivialized.

But some OCO do require physical presence, in the person of an RSCO. The presence of infantry soldiers with RSCO capabilities is at the core of our vision. This is consistent with Cardon's suggested model of a small team tethered to national-level agencies.[7]

---

[6]   Wisniewski, 2016.

[7]   Gould, 2014.

Required Personnel

Just how skilled an RSCO needs to be is, however, an open question. How much of an RSCO's capabilities could be accessed through reachback? How far back does an RSCO have to reach for that support, and how is that support routed, managed, and prioritized? How can RSCOs be integrated into the force and linked with a structure that provides effective and timely reachback? Some tactical OCO might require an on-site expert with sophisticated skills, such as the ability to infiltrate "a local, isolated network that cannot be reached from afar."[8] Other operations might require a human asset to perform physical tasks, such as connecting an alligator clip, splicing a wire, or inserting a thumb drive.

When a human asset is required, there can be no substitute. But, as in the case of inserting a thumb drive, this person might not need to be a full-on "cybergeek." If RSCOs had reachback support, they would likely need significant technological expertise. The tethering model might require up to four types of personnel, each with an associated role, location, and skill level. How many of each type is required varies, as shown in Table 5.1, which shows a split between the levels of expertise needed and used across forward and rear echelon organizations.[9]

Challenges to Be Overcome

In pursuing tactical OCO, the Army might encounter many of the same challenges associated with the use of armed drones, as described in Chapter Four. This includes the vital need for situational aware-

---

[8]   Gould, 2014.

[9]   Based on experiences at Cyber Flag, Cyber Guard, the NSA CDX, Cyber Yankee, and Project C, there appears to be a balance between teams of full-out, highly technical cyber warriors and those with broader operational experience. Whether as part of the "tethered" team or "reachback" resources, there needs to be a clear link to the needs of the supported tactical commander and an appreciation of the challenges his unit faces in accomplishing their mission beyond the cyber realm (Wisniewski, 2016).

Table 5.1
Personnel Roles, Locations, Skill Levels, Quantities, and Examples

Role	Location	Skill Level (Health Care Analogy)	Quantity	Examples
Cyber technician/ operator/ employer (RSCO)	Forward	Medic/Navy corpsman	Many: possibly one per platoon	A fully functional infantryman, perhaps with an additional skill identifier and toolkit that allows RSCO service when needed
Planner	Forward	Hospital manager	Moderate: one per unit/ brigade	Officer on a brigade staff with knowledge of cyber capabilities; manages the relationship between reachback personnel and RSCOs; knows about and manages authorities and approvals
Forward cyber expert	Forward	Nurse (Floating)	Limited	Teams/personnel detached to the brigade level that can be fragmented and organized to lower echelons as needed to carry out full-time cyber-related missions
Reachback cyber expert	Rear	Physician	Few	Tool developers, programmers, etc.

ness. OCO usually require extensive intelligence collection using multiple sources. Preparing for OCO requires operators to find, evaluate, and confirm the proper target while simultaneously guarding against negative second-order effects. An inability to develop a comprehensive intelligence picture was one reason why the United States decided against using OCO during Operation Odyssey Dawn in Libya in 2011. Another reason was because administration officials were unable to resolve the question of whether the President has the power to proceed with such an attack without informing Congress.[10] The uncertainty over proper authorities—combined with a lack of intelligence on potential entry points and susceptible nodes in the Libyan communica-

---

[10] Eric Schmitt and Thom Shanker, "U.S. Debated Cyberwarfare in Attack Plan on Libya," *New York Times*, October 17, 2011.

tions network and on Libyan government radars and missiles—meant passing on OCO in this specific case.[11] However, the uncertainty exhibited in this specific case should not be expected in all cases of military operations, especially those where congressional authority for military action has been secured and a properly defined execute order (EXORD) has been authorized by the President and/or the Secretary of Defense and issued by the Chairman of the Joint Chiefs of Staff. The Chairman of the Joint Chiefs of Staff EXORD "is a record communication that authorizes execution of the COA [course of action] approved by the President or [Secretary of Defense]."[12]

As with armed drones, other concerns include blowback and collateral damage. They can be costly and could occur as a result of cyber operations.[13] They could also open the Army, the U.S. government, or private sector entities to reprisals by state or nonstate actors. In other words, the United States can be the victim of unintended consequences (second- or third-order effects) of conducting tactical cyber operations, especially if these operations result in any of the following: (1) causing an adversary to conduct acts of political violence in the United States or against U.S. targets as a counterattack for tactical cyber operations directed against that enemy; (2) revealing to an ally or adversary that tactical cyber operations were being planned or conducted on or through its territory; or (3) revealing that a capability existed to a major U.S. adversary. Furthermore, unintended effects on civilians or infrastructure could become a public-relations nightmare and undermine immediate efforts and the palatability of future OCO. For these reasons and others, a unit or organization that enables a tight coupling

---

[11] Kallie Fink, John D. Jordan, and James E. Wells, "Considerations for Offensive Cyberspace Operations," *Military Review*, May–June 2014, p. 8.

[12] Execution of an operation "begins when the President decides to use a military option to resolve a crisis" and authorizes an EXORD. EXORDs define "the time to initiate operations and convey guidance not provided earlier" in the planning of a military operation. See discussion of EXORDs in DoD, *Joint Operation Planning*, JP 5-0, August 11, 2011, p. xvi.

[13] Metcalf and Barber, 2014.

between rear and forward echelons—as described in this chapter—could mitigate these challenges.[14]

Discussion: Organization and Personnel Aspects of Tactical OCO

Although cyber operational capability at tactical levels (i.e., corps and below) is not a new concept, cyber operational expertise in the Army remains a scarce resource. This challenge is most apparent at tactical levels, where there are no dedicated, organic capabilities for OCO. As the Army develops concepts, doctrine, and capabilities to support OCO at tactical levels, it must bear this in mind.

---

[14] There are other challenges. The ability to leverage the technology to scale the power of a single cyber operator or small team of cyber operators would be an immense benefit. However, left unchecked, automated capabilities could themselves end up targeting an "off-limits" resource or be used by a sophisticated adversary toward U.S. systems. The potential for "blowback" will need to be considered by not only the "tethered" formations and the "reachback" resources, but by tactical and operational commanders as well (Jeffery Caton, "Complexity and Emergence in Ultra-Tactical Cyberspace Operations," presentation to the Fifth International Conference on Cyber Conflict, Tallinn, Estonia, 2013). One question that is always raised is, "What would happen if this ends up in the hands of a U.S. audience?" (Wisniewski, 2016).

CHAPTER SIX

Choosing Practical Types of Tactical OCO

A number of factors help determine which tactical OCO are practical and mitigate limiting challenges.[1] These effects include proximity, frequency, expertise, and containment (of effects). *Proximity* refers to how physically close a soldier needs to get to a target to employ OCO. *Frequency* refers to how often a tactical unit (e.g., a BCT) expects to perform OCO. *Expertise* refers to the degree to which highly trained experts are required to perform OCO. *Containment* (of effects) refers to the ability to keep OCO effects within a bounded area for a predetermined duration. Note that cyber operations expertise in the Army is a scarce resource. This challenge is most apparent at tactical levels, where there are no dedicated, organic capabilities for OCO.[2]

These four key factors are themselves a function of other circumstances. For example, the determinants of proximity are mission requirements and the vulnerabilities (e.g., accessibility) of the target. The array of missions possible within the full range of operations is quite wide, ranging from domestic aid and foreign humanitarian assistance to high-intensity force-on-force engagements. Expertise, frequency, proximity, and ability to ensure containment will therefore vary widely as well.

---

[1] Tactical echelons include corps, division, brigade, and battalion.

[2] Note that each corresponding staff section below corps and division (e.g., brigade and battalion staff and line company personnel) has a narrower range of collective expertise and fewer experts than its counterparts at higher echelons of command. The ability to find the necessary expertise—both the type and the amount required—organically (i.e., from within the BCT) or within echelons above brigade or JIIM partners will be critical.

The flowchart presented in Figure 6.1 provides a way to assess the practicability of OCO. Arguably, over time, the factors will affect each other. For example, mission requirements could become a function of the availability of expertise, and vice versa. If no appropriately trained personnel are available to execute a particular offensive tactical cyber

Figure 6.1
Flowchart to Assess Practical Tactical Offensive Cyber Capability

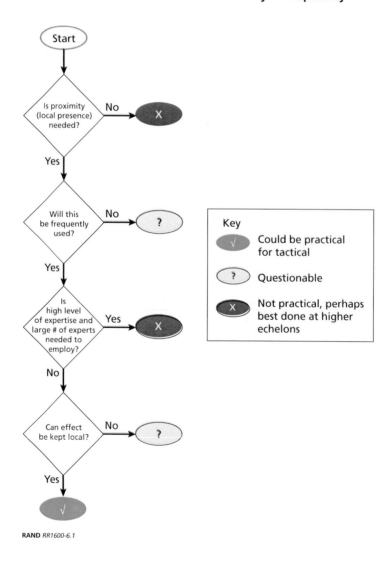

RAND RR1600-6.1

operation, then such missions—even when they would be preferable to alternatives—are less likely to be pursued (or, in the worst case, will not be considered). For the purposes of the flowchart presented, we assume that the four key factors are independent.

To test the soundness of the flowchart, we consider the counter-radio electronic warfare (CREW) device used in Iraq to protect convoys against IEDs (see Figure 6.2). Although CREW was not employed as an offensive weapon, its use of the electromagnetic spectrum to broadcast a jamming signal has both offensive and defensive properties.[3] In respect to proximity, these CREW devices needed to be employed in

Figure 6.2
Jammers Employed at Tactical Levels to Counter IEDs in Iraq

SOURCE: DoD, "Army Creates Electronic Warfare Career Field," Army.mil, February 2006.
RAND RR1600-6.2

---

[3]   The broader area of EW (see Department of the Army, *FM 3-36: Electronic Warfare in Operations*, Washington, D.C.: Headquarters, Department of the Army, October 16, 2012)

the convoys to be effective:[4] Close proximity to the IED trigger was required. In respect to *frequency*, CREW devices were employed constantly to protect convoys and other tactical units on patrol: CREW devices were used frequently. In respect to *expertise*, only some familiarity with CREW was required to be effective; highly trained experts were unnecessary, although planning for their use is more involved than simply turning them on when on patrol. In respect to the *containment of effects*, jamming devices like CREW only impact the local area within proximity to the jammer: the effects lasted for only a fixed period and affected only a small area.

---

is beginning to overlap with cyber operations, as explained in Department of the Army, FM 3-38: Cyber Electromagnetic Activities, Washington, D.C.: Headquarters, Department of the Army, January 30, 2013. This same point is made in Isaac Porche, Christopher Paul, Michael York, Chad C. Serena, Jerry M. Sollinger, Elliot Axelband, Endy M. Daehner, and Bruce J. Held, *Redefining Information Warfare Boundaries for an Army in a Wireless World*, Santa Monica, Calif.: RAND Corporation, MG-1113-A, 2013.

[4]   SRC, "AN/ULQ-35 CREW Duke System," web page, 2015.

CHAPTER SEVEN
Best Practices, Goals, and Strategy

Each of the three case studies described in this report was selected to illuminate one of the following three overarching requirements for tactical OCO:

1. The Army must be able to build trust and operate with JIIM partners (case study one).
2. The Army must be able to employ cyber capabilities at all echelons, including tactical echelons (case study two).
3. The Army must be able to operate with existing authorities and prepared to operate with authorities it might gain in the future (case study three).

This chapter synthesizes lessons learned to arrive at best practices, outlines important considerations, offers associated recommendations, and concludes with a brief examination of doctrine, organization, training, materiel, leadership, personnel, facilities, and policy (DOTMLPF-P) shortfalls associated with the Army's conduct of tactical OCO.

Best Practices and Associated Recommendations

Taken together, the lessons learned from the case studies suggest five best practices for the Army as it develops its ability to conduct and support tactical OCO (Table 7.1). Associated recommendations follow the table.

Table 7.1
Lessons Learned from Case Studies

Lesson Learned	Case Study One: JIATF-S	Case Study Two: USMC Tactical SIGINT	Case Study Three: Armed Drones	Cyber Pilots
1. Respect constraints	Information-sharing rules of participating organizations must be accommodated	Accepting conditions makes it hard for partner to say "no"		
2. Be patient	Relationship building takes time	Preparation makes it possible to seize an opportunity	Title 50 organizations will have dominant roles, must be partners	
3. Operate/ learn by doing	High tempo of operations builds cohesion	Ongoing operations can demonstrate success and trustworthiness	Emerging threats, new capabilities could result in new authorities	Operators' skill is related to hands-on experience with new techniques
4. Seek win-win	Understanding and serving participating organizations' equities are crucial	Understanding and serving a partner's equities are crucial		Operators must understand needs of brigade commander
5. Be there	Collocation increases mutual understanding among participating organizations	Establishing a presence in the partner organization can be instrumental in success		Being physically close to commander is important; common language must be developed and used

Respect Constraints

Current authorities for tactical OCO are both murky and evolving. Until those authorities are clarified and, potentially, devolved to lower echelons, they will remain deliberately granted by and managed at higher (e.g., strategic and operational) echelons. The Army should plan to coordinate with these higher echelons and partner agencies/nations.

Be Patient

Relationship building takes time. The Army cannot expect to immediately have the trust and respect of its JIIM partners—that trust and respect must be earned. The Army should not ask for more than a partner can reasonably be asked to give, especially in the case of new relationships. The Army should accept the need to acquire independence, cooperation, access, and other benefits incrementally rather than instantaneously. Incremental steps and success are self-reinforcing and will lead to greater freedom of action over time. Similarly, repeated failure will undermine existing relationships and place even greater constraints on Army operations and personnel. The Army should therefore address instances of miscommunication and "stepping on toes" quickly and thoroughly. It must be noted that some Army military intelligence brigades already have well-established relationships with key agencies (e.g., the NSA).

Operate/Learn by Doing

Operations (i.e., "doing") give relationships a chance to grow and mature, and they provide opportunities to demonstrate the utility of relationships and willingness to serve partner equities. In the case of military partners, the Army might find that exercises at command posts and at combat training centers afford opportunities for "doing." It must accept, however, that, in nonmilitary organizations, training is not considered doing. Very few non–DoD partners have missions that can be served by a force that is ready but not operating. Many non–DoD partners will expect little benefit from—and therefore have little interest in—offering their personnel to "idle" military formations.

The Army will need to find creative ways for reaping the benefits of "doing" with JIIM partners when BCTs are not deployed. Partner equities will influence how this can be accomplished. A useful example is how the U.S. Navy utilizes a Fleet Intelligence Detachment to maximize "doing." In 2009, Navy Cyber Forces established the Fleet Intelligence Detachment at the Office of Naval Intelligence to improve the training of operational intelligence officers and intelligence specialists with an Imagery Interpretation Naval Enlisted Code. The officers obtain operational intelligence training mostly within Nimitz departments, and the intelligence specialists receive imagery interpretation training primarily prior to deployment. When not deployed, FID personnel integrate within ONI to continue advanced training and provide support.[1]

Similarly, the Army could consider, for example, detaching BCT cyber personnel to work for partners while the BCT is in garrison. During exercises, the detached personnel could return to the formation along with personnel from the partner organization. This would provide the partner a material benefit (i.e., soldiers are detached and working for them) and help build relationships, both through the soldiers' detachment to the partners and through the partner personnel's participation in exercises. (Presumably, these personnel would join the formation during operational deployments.)

Seek Win-Win

When approaching a partner, the Army should make the partnership a "good deal" for that partner up front, which might mean initially subordinating the Army's goals and interests to those of the partner. As the relationship grows, the Army should seek ways to better understand, respect, and serve partner equities whenever possible. The Army should be mindful that partner organizations' rules, values, and objectives might differ from its own. To successfully engage potential JIIM partners, the Army needs to establish protocols for and a culture of ensuring that the goals and objectives of these partners are understood and respected. When it partners on a tactical cyber operation with, for example, the NSA, the Army needs to ensure that the NSA sees the outcome as a "win" for its strategic mission.

Be There

As the Army considers how best to embed capability at tactical echelons, it should identify how to establish and maintain a relationship

---

[1] "Fleet Intelligence Detachment," LinkedIn, web page, March 4, 2014.

between the personnel who will serve at those tactical echelons and the partner agencies and organizations with which they will frequently interact.

The Army should plan to unilaterally provide LNOs in the hope that the "give-to-get" approach will ultimately result in reciprocation. These Army LNOs should be high-caliber, productive staff members that partner organizations are happy to host. When partners send LNOs, the Army should not keep them at arm's length or allow them to languish with no task beyond "liaising." Partner LNOs should be fully integrated when possible, and, at the very least, should be kept busy with important work that shows them how their organization's needs are being served.

The Army is in the process of locating its operational and institutional cyber organizations in close proximity to NSA-Georgia, a decision aimed at creating "tremendous synergy through closer collaboration and coordination."[2] The Army should also consider designing career paths for cyber personnel that rotate them through the NSA's headquarters at Fort Meade and the offices and commands of other relevant JIIM partners.

Authorities Issues

As previously noted, authorities for tactical OCO will remain deliberately granted by and managed at higher (e.g., strategic and operational) echelons in the near term. As case study three highlights, for any capability, concerns regarding blowback, deconfliction, attribution, and proportionality will have to be addressed. Furthermore, any capability employed might need to be preceded by a significant need to collect intelligence. For these reasons, higher echelons must be involved with the application of OCO, along with key partners, e.g., Title 50 organizations.

---

[2]   Kelly Jo Bridgewater, "Commanding General of Army Cyber Command Addresses Chamber of Commerce," *Fort Gordon Signal*, March 7, 2014.

Case study three is also instructive with regard to opportunities. As described in Chapter Three, concerns (perceived and real limitations on authorities, concerns about blowback, controlling for proportionality, and other challenges usually managed at the strategic echelon) regarding USMC conduct of tactical SIGINT were overcome; the same limitations for tactical OCO may be surmounted similarly (as described in the lessons listed in Table 7.1). Furthermore, there are emerging threats and new cyber operational capabilities being developed; pressures stemming from these developments could compel the construction of new authorities especially as mission needs evolve. The bottom line: The successful employment of SIGINT capability with tactical level units in Operation Enduring Freedom projects an opportunity to do the same for certain offensive cyber capabilities.

It is worth noting that in Iraq, the Army placed SIGINT terminal guidance teams at the tactical level (within brigades), which "[used] sophisticated collection equipment to locate and target high-value individuals."[3] That effort was considered effective.[4] What is evident is the opportunity to create cyber versions of those teams, coined by Murray[5] as "cyber terminal guidance" teams, which he illustrates at the bottom of Figure 7.1 (circled as item #2).

Figure 7.1 accounts for a number of important features and noteworthy elements including: higher echelon tie-in, teams to deliver cyber effects via close access, a focus on "local effects," synchronization and coordination between Army units and joint, interagency partners, and most importantly, a clear desire to employ cyber personnel and effects at multiple tactical levels (corps, division, and brigade).

---

[3]   David Sula, "Intelligent Training," *INSCOM Journal*, Winter 2012.

[4]   See Raymond T. Odierno, Nichoel E. Brooks, and Francesco P. Mastracchio, "ISR Evolution in the Iraqi Theater," *Joint Force Quarterly*, No. 50, 3rd Quarter 2008, pp. 51–55.

[5]   Hurcules Murray, "Cyber Requirements," briefing delivered at Armed Forces Communications and Electronics Association TechNet: Achieving Force 2025 Through Signals and Cyber, Augusta, Ga., September 10, 2014.

Figure 7.1
Army Seeks "Cyber/EW Units [That Provide] Timely, Responsive, Continuous Support for Offensive Cyber and EW"

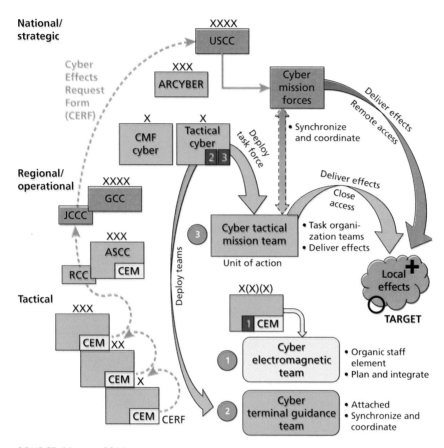

SOURCE: Murray, 2014.
NOTES: CMF = Cyber Mission Force; USCC = United States Cyber Command; GCC = Geographic Combatant Command; JCCC = Joint Cyber Component Command; ASCC = Army Service Component Command; RCC = Regional Cyber Center; CEM = Cyber Electromagnetic Team; CERF = Cyber Effects Request Form; X = Brigade, XX = Division, etc.

RAND *RR1600-7.1*

DOTMLPF-P Changes Needed

As previously noted, cyber operational expertise in the Army is currently scarce and related doctrine and concepts are not yet finalized. Table 7.2 summarizes DOTMLPF-P needs and briefly describes the status of efforts to address those shortfalls.

Table 7.2
Known DOTMLPF-P Needs and Status of Efforts to Address Them

	Needs	Status of Efforts to Address Needs
D	Army offensive tactical cyber operations need to be incorporated into Army doctrine for mission command and operations in cyberspace. The Army currently relies on FM 3-38, *Cyber Electromagnetic Activities*.	The Army is revising FM 3-12, *Cyber Operations and Electronic Warfare*, and FM 3-13, *Inform and Influence Activities*. Additions and modifications to FM 6-0, Army Doctrine Reference Publication 6-0, and Army Doctrine Publication 6-0 should also be considered.
O	The Army needs to develop a structure for reachback, add a cyber officer to brigade staff, develop a structure for forward experts and forward operators, and add RSCOs to the modified table of organization and equipment.	Combat training center rotations are experimenting with augmentees to the brigade and higher headquarters in the form of DSTs using personnel from the CPB and other support personnel from the 780th Military Intelligence Brigade.
T	New training needs must be addressed, including the need for inclusion of cyber effects in more exercises.	The Cyber Center of Excellence is developing a new curriculum. In conjunction, additional specified cyber tasks for FM 7-15, *Army Universal Task List*, should be considered.
M	The Army must continue to acquire and/or develop cyber-specific tools/materiel solutions that support Title 10 functions, such as cyber ISR and cyber OPE.[a] In particular, the Army must also acquire specific tool packs for RSCOs. For all of the above, associated new requirements generation from TRADOC is needed to enable acquisition.	Developments within the Army's Communications-Electronics Research, Development and Engineering Center and Intelligence and Security Command continue.
L	The Army must educate its leadership on cyber operations in order to provoke a cultural change in relation to how cyber operations can be employed.	The Army is currently conducting numerous "Cyber Week" sessions and is planning more leadership education.

Table 7.2—Continued

Needs	Status of Efforts to Address Needs
P	
F	Ranges must incorporate cyber into individual and collective training. More space for Sensitive Compartmented Information Facility (SCIF) is needed.	The Cyber Center of Excellence is examining options for more SCIF space. U.S. Army Communications-Electronics Command is standing up training ranges, which enable remote access.[b]
P	The Army needs clear authorities for offensive operations at tactical levels.	Office of the Secretary of Defense-level considerations are ongoing.

[a] In the context of cyberspace operations, ISR is defined as an "activity that synchronizes and integrates the planning and operation of sensors, assets, and processing, exploitation, and dissemination systems in direct support of current and future operations. This is an integrated intelligence and operations function ... [it can be used as] defensive countercyber." Cyber operational preparation of the environment is defined as "nonintelligence enabling functions within cyberspace conducted to plan and prepare for potential follow-on military operations. This includes but is not limited to identifying data, system/network configurations, or physical structures connected to or associated with the network or system (e.g., software, ports, and assigned network address ranges or other identifiers) for the purpose of determining system vulnerabilities, as well as actions taken to assure access and/or control of the system, network, or data during anticipated hostilities" (James Cartwright, "Joint Terminology for Cyberspace Operations," memorandum for the service chiefs, combatant commanders and directors of Joint Staff directorates, 2010).
[b] Solivan, 2015.

Strategy for Army Tactical Cyber Operations

In this section, we propose a strategy for tactical Army cyber operations. We begin with a vision statement and then we enumerate overarching goals, objectives, and associated activities. As part of this strategy, we describe what the Army, as an institution, needs to do to realize a vision for tactical cyber operations.

Vision Statement

The Army operates effectively in and through cyberspace by attaining the necessary cyber capabilities that can and need to be employed at a tactical level. It uses organic offensive and defensive cyber capabilities at the tactical echelon with dedicated personnel in support of tactical units while operating within existing authorities. It integrates kinetic and nonkinetic effects. It builds trust and operates with JIIM partners, and prepares to operate with authorities that might be gained in the future that permit greater capabilities.

Goals and Objectives for a Strategy for Tactical Army Cyber Operations

Supporting this vision will require a strategy specifically designed to accomplish specific near-term goals and objectives (see Table 7.3).

Defend Tactical Assets and Key Cyber Terrain

According to recent Arroyo Center research, few, if any, doctrinal processes exist that tactical units can use to identify cyber key terrain as a part of mission analysis. Absent commonly understood processes and procedures for this purpose, tactical units either will fail to identify cyber key terrain or will do so in an uncoordinated fashion. In either case, the result will be a failure to appropriately defend tactical assets at critical junctures during the conduct of its mission and/or the misappropriation of crucial and scarce cyber resources and personnel.

Enable Effects Through Tactical Offensive Cyber Operations

Cyber effects (and threats) should not be—and increasingly are not—limited to operational and strategic echelons. Tactical organizations are increasingly the subject of adversary and even nonstate actor cyber operations. Furthermore, there are increasing opportunities associated with the exploitation of cyber by tactical organizations. Tactical organizations, because of their "ownership" of land in an AO, should serve as a bridge between the virtual world of cyber and the physical world of land operations.

Provide the Means to Enable Cyber-Derived Intelligence to Support the Tactical Commander

Increasingly, data and information made available through social media or shared through cyberspace have value to military planners and operators. The Army needs to develop capabilities to process and analyze

Table 7.3
Goals and Objectives

Goal	Objective	Important Task/Activity
1. Defend tactical assets and key cyber terrain	1.1. Actively defend mission command systems used at the brigade level	1.1.1. Apply intrusion detection capability on tactical networks
		1.1.2. Perform research, development, testing, and evaluation on state-of-the-art identity management systems designed for the tactical environment
	1.2. Ensure the cybersecurity of weapons and vehicles	
2. Enable effects through tactical offensive cyber operations	2.1. Provide capability to achieve kinetic effects through cyber operations	2.1.1. Deny/degrade/disrupt enemy communication that uses the "local Internet" and social media for C2 and propaganda
		2.1.2. Detect and deny IEDs along the lines of communication as part of the cyber operations and EW missions
		2.1.3. Provide military deception in support of targeting targeting, e.g., influence enemy to meet at coordinated location
		2.1.4. Counter and exploit adversary manned and unmanned air and ground vehicles
	2.2. Enable nonkinetic effects via tactical cyber operations	2.2.1. Manipulate to control or change the adversary's information systems and/or networks in a manner that supports the commander's objectives
		2.2.2. Spread positive IO messages through cyberspace
		2.2.3. Deliver messaging in support of sowing dissention among adversary
		2.2.4. Conduct offensive SMO
	2.3. Use electronic warfare capability as "delivery platform for precision cyber effects"	

Table 7.3—Continued

Goal	Objective	Important Task/Activity
3. Provide the means to enable cyber-derived intelligence to support the tactical commander	3.1. Use cyber operations capability to support commanders targeting needs	3.1.1. Provide/deliver military deception in support of targeting, e.g., influence enemy to meet at coordinated location
		3.1.2. Provide/deliver military deception in support of targeting, e.g., influence enemy to meet at coordinated location
		3.1.3. Use cyber to develop pattern of life
		3.1.4. Conduct information gathering SMO
	3.2. Map cyberspace of local adversary to support military planning	3.2.1. Perform aerial cyber ISR
4. Integrate cyber planning with other planning processes at tactical level	4.1. Develop common vocabulary for the employment of cyber effects	
	4.2. Develop shared understanding of what cyber effects can be achieved	
	4.3. Integrate cyber into ISR planning activity	
	4.4. Integrate cyber into military decisionmaking process	
5. Utilize reachback capabilities to support OCO and DCO	5.1. Effectively use intelligence support to cyber operations	5.1.1. Utilize digital network analysis capability in support of tactical cyber operations
		5.1.2. Integrate EMIB capabilities
	5.2. Integrate higher echelon cybersecurity capability for network defense	5.2.1. E.g., Enable division information assurance cell to provide oversight, detection and tip capability in support of BCT
		5.2.2. Relay cybersecurity network data to higher echelon analysts

Table 7.3—Continued

Goal	Objective	Important Task/Activity
6. Create sufficient types and numbers of training facilities and the opportunities to use these facilities for the development of tactical cyber capabilities and measures for developing tactical cyber proficiency	6.1. F/T-Proper facilities… to test, train, and exercise tactical cyber capabilities	
	6.2. Training is sufficiently realistic for the tactical environment	6.2.1. Exercise actors use real tools against realistic threats (e.g., hybrid threats)
		6.2.2. Test and exercise networks are loaded with sufficient network activity to replicate real world
		6.2.3. Modern equipment is used during network exercises and includes wired and wireless devices
		6.2.4. Integrate or simulate remote reachback intelligence support in exercises
	6.3. Measures of effectiveness and measures of performance for offensive cyber effects	
7. Develop and leverage required capabilities through partnerships and collaboration		

these data for use by tactical organizations, even if this capability can only be accessed through the employment of reachback capabilities.

Integrate Cyber Planning with Other Planning Processes at the Tactical Level

To gain familiarity with the planning and conduct of cyber operations, tactical units must begin to consider them in the conduct of the operations process. Integrating cyber into the operations process will require staff sections to account for cyber effects and planning considerations during the military decisionmaking process. It will also help to shape processes tailored to incorporating higher-echelon support and new cyber personnel and capabilities.

The cyber and fires communities need to come to a common, shared understanding of what can be achieved through the conduct of tactical cyber operations and how this is to be conveyed to tactical units. Incorporating tactical cyber into the targeting process, developing associated measures of performance and effectiveness, and incorporating this into doctrine and TTPs for use at tactical echelons will expand cyber opportunities and effectiveness when employed.

Use Reachback Capabilities to Support OCO and DCO

While Army units have been using reachback capabilities for many purposes, the Army should expand its capacity for conducting reachback in support of cyber operations. Cyber data are voluminous and often difficult to analyze without sufficient staff and specialized tools, none of which are presently available to BCTs. Creating reachback capability would expand the reach of BCTs, provide an invaluable information gathering and intelligence source, and eliminate many of the challenges associated with authorities, manpower, and time available for cyber operations.

Create Sufficient Training Facilities and Opportunities to Use These Facilities

At present, tactical units have few opportunities to plan, prepare for, or conduct tactical cyber operations. The Army will have to develop dedicated ranges for this purpose or will have to expand the capability of other mission support training facilities currently in use. Without the facilities to plan and train for the conduct of tactical cyber, units will not be able to effectively incorporate it into its other operations.

Develop and Leverage Required Capabilities Through Partnerships and Collaboration

The Army should begin working extensively with joint and interagency partners to develop solutions and best practices for the conduct of tactical cyber operations. Ultimately, tactical Army units will not be conducting cyber operations without the support and/or supervision of external organizations. It must now begin to develop extensive working relationships with these organizations not only to understand shared equities, but to develop shared concepts and practices in what is likely to become a regularly exercised capability at the tactical level.

Future Work

There are certainly other case studies that could be explored in terms of assessing the value of reach, authorities, and other aspects discussed in this report with regard to tactical cyber operations. Tactical psyop has a categorization for specific types of authorities, e.g., white, gray, and black. So, there may be lessons learned for tactical cyber operations that can be learned from tactical psyop.

References

Ackerman, Robert K., "Joint Approach Defines Marine Corps Intelligence," *Signal*, April 2004. As of August 11, 2015:
http://www.afcea.org/content/?q=joint-approach-defines-marine-corps-intelligence

Andress, Jason, and Steve Winterfeld, *Cyber Warfare: Techniques, Tactics and Tools for Security Practitioners*, Waltham, Mass.: Syngress, 2011.

Austin, Greg, "The Pentagon's Law of War for Cyberspace," *Diplomat*, December 22, 2015. As of July 28, 2016:
http://thediplomat.com/2015/12/the-pentagons-law-of-war-for-cyberspace/

Bergan, Peter, and Megan Braun, "Drone Is Obama's Weapon of Choice," CNN, September 5, 2012. As of May 9, 2013:
http://www.cnn.com/2012/09/05/opinion/bergen-obama-drone

Biswas, Masudul, and Carrie Sipes, "Social Media in Syria's Uprising and Post-Revolution Libya: An Analysis of Activists' and Blogger's Online Engagement," *Arab Media and Society*, Vol. 19, Fall 2014, pp. 1–21. As of November 16, 2015:
http://www.arabmediasociety.com/?article=847

Bridgewater, Kelly Jo, "Commanding General of Army Cyber Command Addresses Chamber of Commerce," *Fort Gordon Signal*, March 7, 2014. As of August 11, 2015:
http://www.ftgordonsignal.com/news/2014-03-07/Front_Page/Commanding_general_of_Army_Cyber_Command_addresses.html

Byman, David, "Why Drones Work: The Case for Washington's Weapon of Choice," *Foreign Affairs*, Vol. 92, No. 4, July/August 2013, pp. 32–43.

Cartwright, James, "Joint Terminology for Cyberspace Operations," memorandum for the service chiefs, combatant commanders, and directors of Joint Staff directorates, 2010.

Caton, Jeffery, "Complexity and Emergence in Ultra-Tactical Cyberspace Operations," presentation to the Fifth International Conference on Cyber Conflict, Tallinn, Estonia, 2013. As of September 14, 2016:
https://ccdcoe.org/publications/2013proceedings/caton.pdf

Clarke, Richard, and Robert K. Knake, *Cyber War*, New York: Harper Collins, 2010.

Crane, Alfred C., and Richard Peeke, "Using the Internet of Things to Gain and Maintain Situational Awareness in Dense Urban Environments and Mega Cities," *Small Wars Journal*, February 26, 2016. As of May 16, 2016:
http://smallwarsjournal.com/jrnl/art/using-the-internet-of-things-to-gain-and-maintain-situational-awareness-in-dense-urban-envi

"The Cyber Support to Corps and Below," *Stand-To! The Official Focus of the U.S. Army*, July 16, 2015. As of September 13, 2016:
https://www.army.mil/standto/archive_2015-07-16

Department of Defense, "Army Creates Electronic Warfare Career Field," Army. mil, February 2006. As of October 28, 2016:
https://www.army.mil/e2/-images/2009/02/06/29584/index.html

———, *Dictionary of Military and Associated Terms*, Joint Publication 1-02, November 8, 2010 (as amended through February 15, 2016). As of August 2, 2016:
http://www.dtic.mil/doctrine/new_pubs/jp1_02.pdf

———, *Joint Operation Planning*, Joint Publication 5-0, August 11, 2011.

———, *Cyberspace Operations*, Joint Publication 3-12 (R), February 5, 2013.

———, "Fact Sheet: The Department of Defense (DoD) Cyber Strategy," April 2015a.

———, *Department of Defense Law of War Manual*, Washington, D.C.: Office of General Counsel, Department of Defense, June 2015b.

Department of the Army, *Field Manual 3-36: Electronic Warfare in Operations*, Washington, D.C.: Headquarters, Department of the Army, October 16, 2012.

———, *Field Manual 3-38: Cyber Electromagnetic Activities*, Washington, D.C.: Headquarters, Department of the Army, January 30, 2013.

———, *Field Manual 3-12: Cyberspace and Electronic Warfare Operations*, Washington, D.C.: Headquarters, Department of the Army, forthcoming.

Dion-Schwarz, Cynthia, personal communication with the author, April 4, 2016.

DoD—*See* Department of Defense.

Dycuss, Stephen, *National Security Law*, 3rd ed., New York: Aspen, 2002.

Erwin, Marshall Curtis, *Intelligence Issues for Congress*, Washington, D.C.: Congressional Research Service Report, April 23, 2013.

Federation of American Scientists Intelligence Resource Program, "Counterdrug," web page, January 4, 1998.

Fink, Kallie, John D. Jordan, and James E. Wells, "Considerations for Offensive Cyberspace Operations," *Military Review*, May–June 2014, pp. 4–11.

Fischer, Eric A., Edward C. Liu, John Rollins, and Catherine A. Theohary, *The 2013 Cybersecurity Executive Order: Overview and Considerations for Congress*, Washington, D.C.: Congressional Research Service Report, March 1, 2013.

"Fleet Intelligence Detachment," Linkedin, March 4, 2014. As of August 12, 2014: https://www.linkedin.com/groups/Fleet-Intelligence-Detachment-7471657/about

Fryer-Biggs, Zachary, "DoD Looking to 'Jump the Gap' into Adversaries' Closed Networks," *Defense News*, January 15, 2013.

Gould, Joe, "Ground Commanders with Cyber Skills," *Army Times*, July 1, 2014. As of July 28, 2016: http://www.armytimes.com/story/military/2014/07/16/ ground-commanders-with-cyber-skills/12753001/

Herb, Jeremy, "Fewer Drone Strikes Likely the Result of New Obama Policy, Analysts Say," *The Hill*, May 27, 2013. As of July 28, 2016: http://thehill.com/policy/defense/ 301965-fewer-drone-strikes-the-likely-result-of-new-obama-policy-analysts-say

Hollis, David, "Cyberwar Case Study: Georgia 2008," *Small Wars Journal*, January 6, 2011. As of July 28, 2016: http://smallwarsjournal.com/blog/journal/docs-temp/639-hollis.pdf

Johnston, Patrick B., and Annop K. Sarbahi, "The Impact of U.S. Drone Strikes on Terrorism in Afghanistan and Pakistan," *International Studies Quarterly*, Vol. 60, No. 2, 2016, pp. 203–219. As of July 28, 2016: http://isq.oxfordjournals.org/content/60/2/203

Joint Interagency Task Force South, homepage, undated. As of August 11, 2015: http://www.jiatfs.southcom.mil

Justice, Wayne E., "Overview of Coast Guard Drug and Migrant Interdiction," testimony before the House Committee on Transportation and Infrastructure, Subcommittee on Coast Guard and Maritime Transportation, March 18, 2009.

Koscher, Karl, Alexei Czeskis, Franziska Roesner, Shwetak Patel, Tadayoshi Kohno, Stephen Checkoway, Damon McCoy, Brian Kantor, Danny Anderson, Hovav Shacham, and Stefan Savage, "Experimental Security Analysis of a Modern Automobile," presented at IEEE Symposium on Security and Privacy, Oakland, Calif., May 16–19, 2010.

Kushiyama, Kristen, "Army Looks to Blend Cyber, Electronic Warfare Capabilities on Battlefield," Army.mil, October 29, 2013. As of August 12, 2015: http://www.army.mil/article/113678/ Army_looks_to_blend_cyber__electronic_warfare_capabilities_on_battlefield/

————, "Army to Focus on Cyber Strategy in Tactical Environments," CERDEC Public Affairs, May 11, 2015. As of September 12, 2016:
https://www.army.mil/article/148279/
Army_to_focus_on_cyber_strategy_in_tactical_environments

Lowenthal, Mark M., *Intelligence: From Secrets to Policy*, 5th ed., Los Angeles, Calif.: Sage, 2012.

Markey, Edward, and staff, *Tracking & Hacking: Security & Privacy Gaps Put American Drivers at Risk*, U.S. Senate report, February 2015. As of December 21, 2015:
http://www.markey.senate.gov/imo/media/doc/
2015-02-06_MarkeyReport-Tracking_Hacking_CarSecurity%202.pdf

Martinez, Michael, "U.S. Drone Killing of American al-Awlaki Prompts Legal, Moral Debate," CNN, September 30, 2011. As of August 11, 2015:
http://www.cnn.com/2011/09/30/politics/targeting-us-citizens

Masters, Jonathan, "Targeted Killings," Council on Foreign Relations, February 8, 2013. As of July 10, 2013:
http://www.cfr.org/counterterrorism/targeted-killings/p9627

Matthews, Dylan, "Everything You Need to Know About the Drone Debate, in One FAQ," *Washington Post*, March 8, 2013. As of July 10, 2013:
http://www.washingtonpost.com/blogs/wonkblog/wp/2013/03/08/
everything-you-need-to-know-about-the-drone-debate-in-one-faq/

Mazzetti, Mark, and Matt Apuzzo, "Deep Support in Washington for C.I.A.'s Drone Missions," *New York Times*, April 25, 2015. As of July 28, 2016:
http://www.nytimes.com/2015/04/26/us/politics/
deep-support-in-washington-for-cias-drone-missions.html

Menn, Joseph, "Special Report: U.S. Cyberwar Strategy Stokes Fear of Blowback," Reuters, May 10, 2013. As of July 10, 2013:
http://www.reuters.com/article/2013/05/10/
us-usa-cyberweapons-specialreport-idUSBRE9490EL20130510

Metcalf, Andrew, and Christopher Barber, "Tactical Cyber: How to Move Forward," *Small Wars Journal*, September 14, 2014.

Miller, Greg, "Legal Memo Backing Drone Strike That Killed American Anwar al-Awlaki Is Released," *Washington Post*, June 23, 2014. As of August 11, 2015:
https://www.washingtonpost.com/world/national-security/
legal-memo-backing-drone-strike-is-released/2014/06/23/1f48dd16-faec-11e3-
8176-f2c941cf35f1_story.html

Munsing, Evan, and Christopher J. Lamb, *Joint Interagency Task Force–South: The Best Known, Least Understood Interagency Success*, Washington, D.C.: National Defense University Press, June 2011. As of August 7, 2015:
http://ndupress.ndu.edu/Portals/68/Documents/stratperspective/inss/
Strategic-Perspectives-5.pdf

Murray, Hurcules, "Cyber Requirements," briefing delivered at Armed Forces Communications and Electronics Association TechNet: Achieving Force 2025 Through Signals and Cyber, Augusta, Ga., September 10, 2014.

National Archives, Federal Register, Executive Order 12333, United States Intelligence Activities, December 4, 1981.

National Security Agency, "The National Sigint Operations Center," *Cryptologic Spectrum*, Vol. 9, No. 3, Summer 1979, pp. 4–15.

———, "Mission," web page, April 15, 2011.

———, "Signals Intelligence," web page, March 2, 2015. As of September 13, 2016:
https://www.nsa.gov/what-we-do/signals-intelligence/

NSA—*See* National Security Agency.

Nygard, Bryan J., "Radio Battalion Helps ANGLICO Intercept Insurgents," Marines.mil, June 6, 2011. As of August 11, 2015:
http://www.iimef.marines.mil/News/NewsArticle/tabid/472/Article/528866/radio-battalion-helps-anglico-intercept-insurgents.aspx

Odierno, Raymond T., Nichoel E. Brooks, and Francesco P. Mastracchio, "ISR Evolution in the Iraqi Theater," *Joint Force Quarterly*, No. 50, 3rd Quarter 2008, pp. 51–55.

Office of the Staff Judge Advocate, USAICoE and Ft. Huachuca, Intelligence Law & Instructor Division, "Intelligence Oversight," HUMINT Legal Principles, October 3, 2006.

Paul, Christopher, Jennifer D. P. Moroney, Beth Grill, Colin P. Clarke, Lisa Saum-Manning, Heather Peterson, and Brian Gordon, *What Works Best When Building Partner Capacity in Challenging Contexts?* Santa Monica, Calif.: RAND Corporation, RR-937-OSD, 2015. As of November 18, 2015:
http://www.rand.org/pubs/research_reports/RR937

Perlez, Jane, "Chinese Plan to Kill Drug Lord with Drone Highlights Military Advances," *New York Times*, February 20, 2013. As of August 11, 2015:
http://www.nytimes.com/2013/02/21/world/asia/chinese-plan-to-use-drone-highlights-military-advances.html?_r=0

Porche, Isaac, "The Myth of Cyber Defense: What Happens When the Worm Turns," presented at Cyberspace: Malevolent Actors, Criminal Opportunities and Strategic Competition, Panel II: Strategic Competition in Cyberspace Part 2, University of Pittsburgh, November 1–2, 2012.

———, "The Threat from Inside . . . Your Automobile," in Phil Williams and Dighton Fiddner, eds., *Cyberspace: Malevolent Actors, Criminal Opportunities, and Strategic Competition*, Carlisle, Pa.: U.S. Army War College Press, 2016. As of September 13, 2016:
http://www.strategicstudiesinstitute.army.mil/pdffiles/PUB1319.pdf

Porche, Isaac, Christopher Paul, Michael York, Chad C. Serena, Jerry M. Sollinger, Elliot Axelband, Endy M. Daehner, and Bruce J. Held, *Redefining Information Warfare Boundaries for an Army in a Wireless World*, Santa Monica, Calif.: RAND Corporation, MG-1113-A, 2013. As of December 18, 2015: http://www.rand.org/pubs/monographs/MG1113.html

Porche, Isaac, Jerry Sollinger, and Shawn McKay, *A Cyberworm That Knows No Boundaries*, Santa Monica, Calif.: RAND Corporation, OP-342-OSD, 2011. As of November 4, 2016: http://www.rand.org/pubs/occasional_papers/OP342.html

Public Law 107-40, Authorization for Use of Military Force, September 18, 2001.

Quinn, Kristin, "C4ISR Journal Announces Award Winners," *DefenseNews*, October 15, 2010.

Sanger, David E., and Thom Shanker, "Broad Powers Seen for Obama in Cyberstrikes," *New York Times*, February 3, 2013. As of July 28, 2016: http://www.nytimes.com/2013/02/04/us/broad-powers-seen-for-obama-in-cyberstrikes.html

Schmitt, Eric, and Thom Shanker, "U.S. Debated Cyberwarfare in Attack Plan on Libya," *New York Times*, October 17, 2011. As of September 14, 2016: http://www.nytimes.com/2011/10/18/world/africa/cyber-warfare-against-libya-was-debated-by-us.html

Schmitt, Michael N., "International Law in Cyberspace: The Koh Speech and Tallinn Manual Juxtaposed," *Harvard International Law Journal*, Vol. 54, December 2012, pp. 15–16.

Seffers, George I., "Blog: Future Army May Need Offensive Cyber Operations at the Tactical Edge," *Signal*, September 9, 2014. As of August 11, 2015: http://www.afcea.org/content/?q=future-army-may-need-offensive-cyber-operations-tactical-edge

Serena, Chad C., *It Takes More than a Network: The Iraqi Insurgency and Organizational Adaptation*, Stanford, Calif.: Stanford University Press, 2014.

Solivan, Douglas A., "Communications-Electronics Cyber Training Range Launches," *Fort Gordon Globe*, July 10, 2015. As of January 3, 2016: http://www.army.mil/article/150996/Communications_Electronics_Command_cyber_training_range_launches/

SRC, "AN/ULQ-35 CREW Duke System," web page, 2015. As of August 11, 2015: http://www.srcinc.com/what-we-do/ew/crew-duke.html

Stavridis, James, "The New Triad," *Foreign Policy*, June 20, 2013. As of September 13, 2016: http://foreignpolicy.com/2013/06/20/the-new-triad/

Stutser, J. Dana, "China Now Considering Drone Strikes in Its Drug War," *Foreign Policy*, February 19, 2013. As of August 12, 2015:
http://foreignpolicy.com/2013/02/19/
china-now-considering-drone-strikes-in-its-drug-war/

Sula, David, "Intelligent Training," *INSCOM Journal*, Winter 2012. As of May 3, 2015:
https://www.inscom.army.mil/Journal/2012/Winter12/12winter4.html

TRADOC—*See* U.S. Army Training and Doctrine Command.

Treverton, Gregory, *Covert Action: The Limits of Intervention in the Postwar World*, New York: Basic Books, 1987.

U.S. Army Cyber Command, "LandCyber White Paper: 2018–2030," Ft. Meade, Md., September 9, 2013.

———, "Integration of Cyberspace Capabilities into Tactical Units," Army.mil, 2016. As of September 19, 2016:
https://www.army.mil/article/163156/
integration_of_cyberspace_capabilities_into_tactical_units

U.S. Army Training and Doctrine Command, "United States Army Cyberspace Operations Concept Capability Plan 2016–2028," U.S. Army Training and Doctrine Command Pamphlet 525-7-8, February 22, 2010.

———, "Enabling Operations in Cyberspace Through Institutional and Operational Unity of Effort White Paper," July 9, 2013.

———, "The U.S. Army Operating Concept: Win in a Complex World 2020–2040," Pamphlet 525-3-1, October 31, 2014.

U.S. Constitution, Article II, §§ 2–3.

U.S. Marine Corps, "Marine Cryptologic Support Battalion Intelligence Department," undated. As of August 11, 2015:
http://www.hqmc.marines.mil/intelligence/Units/
MarineCryptologicSupportBattalion.aspx

U.S. Marine Corps Concepts and Programs, "Tactical Signals Intelligence (SIGINT) Collection System (TSCS)," web page, 2015.
https://marinecorpsconceptsandprograms.com/programs/
intelligence-surveillance-and-reconnaissance/tactical-signals-intelligence-sigint

Wall, Andru, "Demystifying the Title 10-Title 50 Debate: Distinguishing Military Operations, Intelligence Activities, & Covert Action," *Harvard National Security Journal*, Vol. 3, No. 1, September 2011, pp. 85–143. As of August 11, 2015:
http://www.soc.mil/528th/PDFs/Title10Title50.pdf

White House, *International Strategy for Cyberspace: Prosperity, Security and Openness in a Networked World*, Washington, D.C., May 2011. As of May 5, 2015:
https://www.whitehouse.gov/sites/default/files/rss_viewer/
international_strategy_for_cyberspace.pdf

Wisniewski, Brian, personal communication with the author, February 29, 2016.